WALKING
in the FAITH *of the*
SON *of* GOD

MARC BAKER

TWO BLESSED BEARS PUBLISHING
Bradenton, FL

Walking in the Faith of the Son of God
ISBN: 979-8-9887462-2-5 (paperback)
ISBN: 979-8-9887462-3-2 (eBook)
Copyright © 2023 by Marc Baker
Bradenton, FL 34203

Published by:
Two Blessed Bears Publishing
Bradenton, FL 34203

www.mbmediaministries.net

I am crucified with Christ: nevertheless I live; yet not I, but Christ liveth in me: and the life which I now live in the flesh I live by the faith of the Son of God, *who loved me, and gave himself for me.*

GALATIANS 2:20, KJV
(emphasis added)

Contents

Chapter 1

The Measure of Faith

For I say, through the grace given to me, to everyone who is among you, not to think of himself more highly than he ought to think, but to think soberly, as God has dealt to each one a measure of faith.

ROMANS 12:3

I recognize that innumerable books have been written about the subject of faith. This is a topic that most Christians are hungry to learn about. Whole ministries, churches, and even denominations have been built around the subject. Kenneth E. Hagin is often referred to as the father of the modern faith movement, as his primary message was faith. He paved a trail for us to follow with the faith message. This does not mean we should focus on him or the messages he preached. We are to be led by the Spirit of God (Romans 8:14), and He will always help us keep our eyes on Jesus, who is "the author and finisher" of the measure of faith God has deposited in our spirits (Hebrews 12:2).

I spent some time discussing this book with the Holy Spirit before I agreed to write it. He reminded me of my struggles with the faith message when I first heard it almost thirty years ago. I can look back now and see that this was largely due to the way many ministers I sat under taught faith. It was not that they were teaching in error; rather, it was how they presented the subject. There were so many seven-step lists, formulas, and methods, and they all ran together. Some ministers would give us seven steps to mountain-moving faith, and others would offer a formula for world-overcoming faith. They were talking about moving mountains and overcoming the world, but I would have been satisfied with faith that could move an anthill!

So, what is different about this book that makes it unique in my mind? To start with, I will not give you any lists or formulas. I have learned that faith grows out of relationship with the Word of God and the Holy Spirit. Our ability to operate in the faith of God is dependent on our relationship with Him. Secondly, I've heard many ministers talk about the size of our faith. I am not going to be one of those. The Bible clearly tells us that God has given every person the measure of His faith (Romans 12:3). We have the same measure of faith the early church walked in. Paul tells us in Galatians 2:20 that he lived life by the faith of the Son of God. This infers that the faith he walked in was the same faith Jesus operated in, which makes sense, as Jesus only did the things that pleased God (John 8:29), and it is only possible to please God when we are operating in faith (Hebrews 11:6).

The Greek word translated as "faith" in Romans 12:3, Galatians 2:20, and Hebrews 11:6 refers to faith that is always received as a gift given by God. This is a type of faith that cannot be produced through human effort. If it was sufficient for Jesus to raise Lazarus from the dead (John 11:38–44), heal the woman with an issue of blood (Mark 5:25–34), and walk on water during a storm (Matthew 14:22–33), I would think it is also sufficient for us to overcome any trial or situation experienced during our Christian journey.

The Faith of the Son of God

One of the hardest things I had to overcome when I first started meditating on faith was the concept that God does not expect us to use our natural human faith to access His blessings. He recognized the limitations of it and gave us a measure of His faith to use and operate in instead. As I mentioned earlier, the Greek word most often translated as "faith" in the New Testament refers to something we cannot produce. It is always given as a gift from God. Paul points to the need for humility when approaching faith in Romans 12:3:

> For I say, through the grace given to me, to everyone who is among you, not to think *of himself* more highly than he ought to think, but to think soberly, *as God has dealt to each one a measure of faith.* (Emphasis added in latter half of verse)

For clarity, I will refer to God's faith as "the measure of faith" throughout this book. This is to help you differentiate between your natural human faith and the faith you received from God. In practice, many people refer to their faith when they are speaking of God's faith. We must avoid the temptation to become legalistic in this area. I differentiate between the two types of faith in this book to help you understand which is being referenced. I find it also helps to do this in my mind whenever I step out in a faith project because it eliminates the urge to lean on my efforts to access the things I am expecting to receive from God. This has enabled me to rest in Him during my faith journey, and I believe it will allow you to do the same.

Growing My Faith versus Growing into His Faith

I have heard many ministers speak of ways to grow our faith over the years. The emphasis always seems to be on the effort we put into causing that growth to happen. Let's take a moment to think about this concept of growing our faith. If God has given us a measure of His faith, does it make sense that He would only give us a small measure and then expect us to grow it from there? I don't think so. That is why I struggled so much to understand how to operate in faith. I was always dwelling on the things I could do to become stronger in faith. In other words, I was focused on myself instead of on God. The Holy Spirit was patient and helped me see that God did not expect me to grow the faith He had given me. He only expected me to grow into it. There is a vast difference. Growing into His faith involves spending quality time with His Word and the Holy Spirit. It is impossible to succeed in our faith walk without first becoming grounded in Scripture and developing our relationship with the Spirit. You will find that I constantly refer to this relationship in this book.

I fell into the trap of comparing my faith with every minister I sat under. Mine always fell short. This led me into a works mentality. I exhausted myself trying to get faith to work for me like it did for the great men and woman of God who had come before me. I spent hundreds of dollars on books about faith, but I just could not get it to work like it did for the people I read about. The Holy Spirit finally got my attention and showed me that the only difference between a minister like Kenneth E. Hagin and myself was the amount of time and dedication that was put into learning how to operate in God's faith. He dedicated countless hours in his early years to meditating in the Word and developing his relationship with the Holy Spirit. Dr. Hagin operated in faith from a foundational relationship with the Word and the Spirit. We can do the same thing. Words cannot begin to express the relief I experienced at the realization that I had enough faith and did not have to worry about increasing it. Instead, I only had to commit time to developing my relationship with the Word and the Spirit, as those who I had been reading about had done.

God has given every person a measure of His faith. We do not have to earn it. The only requirement to receive it is hearing His Word (Romans 10:17). The Holy Spirit uses the Word to birth God's faith in the human spirit. It is given to us by God to use without limitation. Growing into His faith requires us to spend time meditating in the Word of God and developing our relationship with the Holy Spirit. A relationship requires commitment, and we must commit to spending time every day with the Word and the Spirit. You cannot consistently walk in faith without also consistently spending time meditating in Scripture. As mentioned earlier, our success or failure boils down to our relationship with the Word and the Spirit. The Holy Spirit was sent to reveal Jesus to us, but He will not do so outside of the Word of God. He also cannot teach us if we are too busy to spend time with Him.

Paul left us instructions on how to receive God's faith in Romans 10:17 (KJV): "So then faith cometh by hearing, and hearing by the word of God." The Greek word translated as "faith" in this verse is *pistis*. It describes a faith that is always a gift from God—a faith that can never be produced through human effort. I had exhausted myself trying to grow my faith through self-effort because I was ignorant of this truth. The faith Paul is speaking of is a gift from God. It is the same faith God exercised in creation (Genesis 1). Jesus made us worthy to receive God's faith through His death, burial, and resurrection. The Lord is "the author and finisher" of the measure of faith God has given to every person (Hebrews 12:2). We must never forget that Jesus' redemptive work will always be the foundation on which our faith walk is built. It is impossible for any person to receive God's measure of faith without first being cleansed by the blood of Jesus.

There are two other words in Romans 10:17 that we need to look at. First, the Greek word translated as "by" has a two-layered meaning. It represents something that moves from the interior outward. God's measure of faith functions at the spiritual level and moves outward through our soul and into our body. The second word is "hearing." It points to the ear of our spirit, referring to an inner hearing that is associated with receiving faith from God. The Holy Spirit communicates revelation directly to our spirits, and this is how the measure of faith is received. This communication occurs as we spend time meditating in the written Word. We will look at these two words in greater depth and explore how the process of faith begins as hope, moves into vision, and then finally becomes operational as the faith of God. I mention it here only for introduction.

Our Hopeless State

Our natural human faith is inadequate to even receive salvation. Humanity was left in a hopeless state as a result of sin. God recognized this and gave us a measure of His faith. The Holy Spirit was active when we heard the gospel. He transmitted God's faith into our spirit in the form of an incorruptible seed (1 Peter 1:23). The seed developed roots in our souls, releasing the full power of God's measure of faith. Our ability to believe in Jesus' redemptive work grew from this faith, leading us to confess Him as our Lord and Savior. According to Romans 10:10, we were saved at that moment. Our spirits were recreated, and we became new creations (2 Corinthians 5:17) sealed in Christ Jesus by the Holy Spirit (Ephesians 1:13).

I struggled with faith in my early years because my whole paradigm was wrong. The reason for this was the teaching I had received. I was told "my" faith failures were a result of "my" faith not being strong enough. This placed me into what seemed like a never-ending cycle of works-based effort that left me exhausted and ready to quit. The Holy Spirit finally got through the cloud I was living under and showed me that I could rest. I already had the measure of faith in my spirit and had used it to receive salvation. The Spirit helped me see that my efforts were not accomplishing anything. He helped me learn to get off the proverbial hamster wheel of self-effort and taught me to rest in the faith that God had already put into my spirit. He will help you just as He helped me.

An Equal Measure of Faith

God has given us His measure of faith (Romans 12:3). This is a truth that seems to be widely missed in the church today. He gave us His faith to receive salvation, and to use each day as we walk out our Christian journey. Peter refers to the measure of faith in 2 Peter 1:1:

> Simon Peter, a bondservant and apostle of Jesus Christ,
> *To those who have obtained like precious faith with us* by the righteousness of our God and Savior Jesus Christ. (Emphasis added)

"Faith" is once again translated from the Greek word *pistis* in this verse. This is the same word that Paul used in Romans 10:17. It refers to a faith that is always received as a gift from God. God's measure of faith is available to any person who will receive it. They will only know this is possible, though, by first hearing the Word of God. We cannot receive any of God's gifts without first gaining knowledge transmitted to our spirit by the Holy Spirit. This includes His measure of faith. The Spirit will never work separate from the Word of God. As mentioned previously, everything in the Christian life flows out of a relationship with the Word and the Spirit. He has shown me that it is impossible to develop any greater level of intimacy with Him than the level of intimacy we've first developed with the Word of God. The opposite is also true. We cannot develop a higher level of intimacy with the Word than we've developed with the Spirit.

The phrase "like precious" in 2 Peter 1:1 implies that this faith is consistent and holds an equal value. In other words, your favorite preacher received a measure of faith equal to yours. God will never

give anyone a greater measure of His faith than He's given to someone else. This does not mean, though, that some people have learned
to operate in the measure of faith given to them at greater levels than
others. The difference is not the quantity or quality of faith received;
rather, it is the time spent developing themselves in the measure of
faith given to them by God through His Word. You can develop yourself in faith to operate at the same levels of God's faith as any other
Christian. This includes great men and women of God throughout
church history, such as Charles Finney or Smith Wigglesworth.

Growing into Your Measure of Faith

Jesus told His disciples the Holy Spirit would join them when He went
away. He promised the Spirit would take His place as their Comforter
and would guide them into all truth when He came (John 16:12–15).
The Holy Spirit lives in the spirit of every Christian. He is standing
by to help us, and He desires to reveal Jesus to us through the Word
of God. He will not force Himself on us, though, and is standing by
waiting for our invitation. I have found it helpful to think of Him
as my teacher and myself as His student in the School of the Spirit.
He was sent to train us. I have found that during our times of fellowship, there is nothing He enjoys more than revealing Jesus in the
Word to me. The Word of God is His assigned textbook for our class
sessions. The Spirit always expects me to bring my Bible to class and
has even given me many reading assignments. His lessons almost
always include homework sourced in the Word!

Paul tells us that the gospel he preached was received through the
revelation of Jesus Christ (Galatians 1:12). This revelation was received
in the School of the Spirit. The Holy Spirit's goal is to move us into a
position of belief to activate the power of God in our lives. He is the
one who taught Paul, and He is the one who will teach us. Unfortunately, Satan has successfully convinced many Christians that the

Holy Spirit is just some intangible force that manifests in our services. This is a lie. He is the third person of the Godhead who was sent to reveal Jesus to us. The Spirit of God wants to spend time with you to develop a relationship. If you haven't met Him yet, I encourage you to set aside time to be alone with Him. He deserves your full attention. Turn off your phone, computer, and television. Ask Him to reveal Himself to you and He will. I have discovered that He even looks forward to the time we spend together!

You will find the Holy Spirit waiting to reveal Himself to you if you just make time for Him. He will teach you how to walk in the measure of faith given to you by God. I think of faith as the foundational subject taught by Him in the School of the Spirit. There is almost universal agreement regarding the power available to us through faith. It is only through revelation knowledge received from the Spirit during our time with Him that we will be able to tap into this power. Revelation knowledge can only be received during time spent alone with the Word and the Spirit. It cannot be accessed through self-effort. We can "acquire" knowledge by studying and memorizing verses, but we cannot enter into revelation knowledge without the help of the Holy Spirit. I did not understand this in my early years, and I found my faith was always so difficult for me due to my lack of relationship with the Spirit. He was sent to teach us but is limited in His ability to do so when we do not recognize His presence in our lives. Everything changed for me when I acknowledged that He was with me and began to spend time with Him. I am sure it will for you too.

The writer of Hebrews accused his readers of being unskillful in the Word of righteousness (Hebrews 5:12). It appears that he was writing to people who were not new Christians. They should have grown in their relationship with the Word and the Spirit to the point that they could teach others. In other words, they had been serving

God for some time and had become established in their local congregations. It is not enough to just receive Jesus and show up week after week for service. You must also become skilled in the Word of God if you are going to develop in the measure of faith. This will not happen, though, if you do not acknowledge the Holy Spirit and give Him time each day to reveal Jesus to you. We cannot grow in our ability to operate in the measure of faith without first growing in our relationship with the Word and the Spirit. As I mentioned earlier in this section, you can "acquire" knowledge about God but not access the power of faith without an impartation of revelation knowledge from the Spirit of God, which cannot happen if we are not spending time with Him.

The Root Issue

Our society is filled with noise. There are hundreds of television channels to choose from, real-time access to news events as they happen, and social media channels to keep up with. We also have family responsibilities, deadlines at work, and social gatherings to attend. If this is not enough, our churches have an almost endless list of volunteer opportunities. I am not saying that it is wrong to volunteer at church, but I am warning you to be mindful of the Spirit's leading. It is far too easy to fall into the trap of allowing all of our time to be lost to distractions, leaving no time left to spend with the Holy Spirit. I have met many wonderful people over the years who have become so busy in their "church" activities that they've left no time for fellowshipping with the Word and the Spirit. Their intentions are good, but even so, they struggle in their Christian journey just as I did in my early years, before I learned of the relationship available to me with the Word and the Spirit.

Hosea tells us that God's people in his day were destroyed due to their lack of knowledge (Hosea 4:6). Jesus told His disciples that

Satan's goal is to steal, kill, and destroy (John 10:10). In the context of our discussion, I believe that Satan has been successful in His efforts to rob the church of her revelation of God's measure of faith and how to operate in it. This has enabled him to achieve the goals that Jesus listed in far too many lives. I believe the primary tools he uses are the distractions mentioned in the previous paragraph. Christians are far too distracted from their relationship with the Word and the Spirit by the busyness of our world. The result is that we are being destroyed for our lack of knowledge, just as the people of Hosea's day were.

I have spent some time over the years discussing these things with the Holy Spirit. He has helped me recognize that the root issue of our lack of power today is our ignorance of God's Word. We have fallen into Satan's trap by allowing ourselves to be distracted by the busyness of life, and as a result, we are not cultivating a relationship with the Word of God and the Spirit. Far too many Christians I've met over the years have settled into a minimal Christian life that is far below the one planned for them by God. The only cure that will change our current situation is for us to become committed to spending time each day with the Word of God and the Holy Spirit. This is the only way we will successfully begin to operate in the measure of faith that has been given to us by God.

I am thankful for the time I've been blessed to spend with the Holy Spirit over the years. He has always been patient and personalized His lessons to my learning style, and He will do the same for you. Our discussions always seem to have the faith received from God woven into them. The Spirit has used our time together to continually lead me into a deeper revelation of Jesus Christ. The knowledge imparted by the Holy Spirit cannot be obtained from self-effort. You can spend hours memorizing Scripture, but if that is all you do, the Word will never form deep roots in your soul. It takes dedicated time and effort to develop your relationship with the Holy Spirit and the Word of God.

We have all been trained by society to look for shortcuts to get things done faster. One of the most important lessons I pray you learn while reading this book is that there are none when it comes to the spiritual realm. Paul tells us that transformation can only come through the renewing of the mind (Romans 12:2). Our goal in the pages ahead is to learn how to operate in God's measure of faith. This will not happen if we are unwilling to turn off our devices and shut ourselves away, out of sight, to be alone with the Spirit and the Word. It is only in these times of separation that any of us can truly experience intimacy with Him at the level He desires. If you eliminate the distractions in your life and develop your relationship with the Spirit, you will grow into the faith that God has given you.

Chapter 2

Pushing beyond
the Mediocre

So then faith comes *by hearing, and hearing by the word of God.*

ROMANS 10:17

Our natural human faith is limited to what it can perceive through
our five physical senses. God understands this. He knew our
limitations and gave us a measure of His faith to overcome them.
This is the same faith that Paul wrote about in Romans 10:17. Peter
also referenced it in 1 Peter 1:3. It is a gift from God that cannot be
produced through human effort (Ephesians 2:8). We can only access
God's measure of faith through His Word. It is made available to
us through Christ's redemptive work on the cross. Paul tells us in
Romans 6:4 that we can "walk in newness of life" when we turn to
God through the death, burial, and resurrection of Christ. If you
have never invited Jesus to be your Savior, I encourage you to do so
now. You only need to believe in your heart and confess Him as your
Lord (Romans 10:10), and He will do the rest.

The Old Testament saints were limited in that they could only
operate in their natural human faith. They did not have access to
the redemptive work of Christ as we do today. Even though they
were spiritually dead, they still accomplished great things when

walking in obedience to God's direction. Hebrews 11 provides a list of some of the exploits they were able to accomplish. Think about how much more we should be doing now that we can access God's measure of faith and are no longer limited to our natural human faith as they were. I sometimes wonder if this is the reason Jesus told His disciples they would do greater works than had been seen in His ministry (John 14:12). He operated under the old covenant. We operate in the new covenant and have been given a measure of God's faith.

The Inner Ear of Our Spirit

I have heard many messages over the years on the importance of listening to the Word of God. The majority always seem to focus on hearing with our physical ears. The Holy Spirit has spoken to me through many of these messages. Very few of them mentioned the inner ear of our spirit. I believe the reason is that we tend to be more aware of the physical realm rather than the spiritual. It is only natural, then, that we would interpret Romans 10:17 this way. We need to take a deeper look at this verse. Is it really focused on faith coming only because of hearing the Word of God with our physical ears? I believe there is a deeper meaning that we have missed.

The Greek word translated as "hearing" in Romans 10:17 is *akoe*. It refers to hearing with our inner ear. There is a vast difference between our spiritual and physical ears. Jesus told the woman at the well in Samaria that God is a Spirit, and His children would worship Him "in spirit and truth" (John 4:24). We are created in His image: spirit, soul, and body (1 Thessalonians 5:23). Paul described the new birth as the point in which our spirit becomes a new creation in Christ Jesus (2 Corinthians 5:17). Our spirit is recreated the moment we confess Jesus as Lord and are born again (Romans 10:10). This is the reason we can walk in newness of life (Romans 6:4). Our spirits are new creations in Christ, which means our entire spiritual nature has been recreated by God.

I mentioned the inner ear and need to elaborate further. We see in John 20:22 that Jesus breathed the Holy Spirit into the disciples during His first appearance to them after being raised from the dead. This was the moment they were born again. Their spirits were recreated, and the Spirit of God took up residence inside of them, just as He resides in us today. Paul tells us that the Holy Spirit lives inside of the Christian's spirit (Romans 8:9). Our soul (mind, will, intellect, and emotions) and body are not affected by the new birth, so the Spirit cannot dwell in them because they are still corrupted. James tells us that the soul is "saved" when the Word of God is fed into it (James 1:21).

Peter describes the Word as an incorruptible seed (1 Peter 1:23). We "plant" this seed in our soul by hearing it with our physical ears and looking at it with our physical eyes. The Word of God must be planted and then given time to develop deep roots in our souls (James 1:21). Paul calls this process the renewing of our minds (Romans 12:2). We are responsible to present our bodies to God (Romans 12:1) and then to feed the Word "seed" into our souls. The rest of the work is done by the Holy Spirit. He will take the planted seed and impart revelation knowledge into our spirits through what I call the ears of the spirit. This is why I believe the Greek word translated as "hearing" in Romans 10:17 refers to an inner ear—the ear of the spirit through which the Holy Spirit imparts revelation knowledge using the Word seeds we have planted in our souls.

Knowledge and Relationship

Peter tells us that we have each received "like precious faith" (2 Peter 1:1). The Greek word translated as "like precious" refers to something with a consistent value in comparison to something else. In this case, he was comparing his faith to that of his readers. Faith, as used in this verse, is always received as a gift from God (Ephesians 2:8). It is the same faith Paul referred to in Romans 10:17 that is transmitted to the human spirit by the Holy Spirit using the incorruptible seed of God's Word. John tells us that any person who claims to live in Christ must walk as He did (1 John 2:6). He was talking about the way we conduct our daily lives. Paul tells us that we are to do this by faith (2 Corinthians 5:7) using the same Greek word as Peter used for faith in 2 Peter 1:1. Therefore, Peter, John, and Paul all exhorted their readers to conduct their lives using a faith that can only be received as a gift from God. I believe this instruction applies equally to us today.

John exhorted His readers to conduct their lives following the example of Christ (1 John 2:6). Taken in combination with Paul's exhortation for us to conduct our lives by faith (2 Corinthians 5:7), I believe we can comfortably say that Jesus lived and operated by faith in His life and ministry. If you do not yet agree with me based on the statements of Peter, Paul, and John, consider the fact that Jesus told His disciples He always did what pleased the Father (John 8:29). The author of Hebrews tells us that it is impossible to please God without faith (Hebrews 11:6). Do you think Jesus could have done only those things that pleased God if He was not operating in faith?

We have been given a measure of God's faith and are expected to operate in it. I believe this is the reason the Lord told His disciples that they would not only be able to do the same miraculous works that He did but also greater ones (John 14:12). He knew His death, burial, and resurrection would open the door for the Holy Spirit to birth His measure of faith directly into the human spirit. The Spirit did this when we heard the gospel and then enabled us to receive salvation using the faith He had deposited in our spirit. This faith was not given by God to just enable us to be born again. It is available to us every moment of every day. Paul understood this and told us that the

Christian life is to be lived "by the faith of the Son of God" (Galatians 2:20, KJV). This is a much greater level of faith than what was available to the Old Testament saints. However, it cannot be consistently accessed if we are not spending time each day meditating in Scripture and fellowshipping with the Spirit of God. Once again, we see that everything flows out of our relationship with the Word and the Spirit.

Faith and Power

I believe salvation is the greatest miracle any person will ever experience. Our Christian journey began with an expression of God's power that raised us from spiritual death to life. God has given us His measure of faith and His Spirit to enable us to walk in the miraculous. The same Holy Spirit who raised Jesus from the grave (Romans 8:11) is living in the spirit of every Christian. He is the one who God anointed Jesus with (Acts 10:38). He is the one who anoints us today (1 John 2:20). This means we have access to the same power that manifested in the ministry of Jesus, the apostles, and the early church. The measure of faith from God is the tool He has given us to unlock it.

Unfortunately, the majority of Christians I've met lack revelation knowledge of these truths. I believe one of the main reasons for this is a lack of correct teaching. Some may have studied these truths and acquired knowledge in their head about them. They may know what their favorite preacher or commentary says, but there is a vast difference between knowledge gained through our efforts and that which is imparted by the Holy Spirit. Revelation knowledge is revealed to us directly by the Spirit. It seems, though, that only the minority of Christians I've met over the years have committed themselves to putting in the time and effort to develop their relationship with Him to the point where they would be capable of moving from knowledge acquired through self-effort into revelation knowledge. This is not a criticism of these people. I've met a lot of good people over the years who knew about the Holy Spirit. Only a few seemed to know they could develop an intimate relationship with Him. In my mind, those of us in the ministry are to blame for the lack of knowledge about His ministry in the church today. I have asked Him about this issue, and He responded with Mark 7:13:

> "… *making the word of God of no effect through your tradi-tion which you have handed down.* And many such things you do." (Emphasis added)

It has been approximately two thousand years since Jesus said these words to His disciples. He was referring specifically to the Jew-ish traditions of His day that had developed since Moses had received the Law. In context, Jesus was specifically speaking of the Pharisees' statements about His disciples not washing their hands before eating. There were many other traditions taught in the synagogues that were not based in Scripture, just as there are today. I do not have room in this book to cover them but recommend you do a search online. You will find a lot of references that describe them.

We may not want to admit it, but most of us are just as guilty today as the Jews of Jesus' day with the traditions we've allowed to infiltrate our ranks. You may not necessarily picture some of our beliefs as being traditions. Examples include statements about sick-ness being the will of God, sickness being a tool used by God to teach His children humility, or the church maturing beyond the need for the miraculous today. Statements like these are usually said by well-meaning ministers or Christians who are just repeating what they have been taught. They do not know any better. I refer to these beliefs as tradition because they cause people to question God's willingness to provide for their need. Many Christians have been hindered in their ability to believe God as a result.

The Same Faith, Authority, and Power

If we have a measure of God's faith available to us, why are we not walking in the same level of anointing that Jesus and the early church walked in? This is a question I've asked many times over the years. The Holy Spirit always pointed me to John 17:3 when I asked it, which seemed like He was ignoring the question. In my mind, the verse did not have anything to do with the power of God. The Holy Spirit has shown me that it does. In the verse, Jesus defines eternal life as knowing God. The Greek word translated as "know" refers to an intimacy achieved through personal firsthand experience with another person. You cannot develop any level of intimacy with a person without first spending time with them. This is true of our natural relationships, and it is also true of our relationship with God. Jesus told His disciples that He only did the things that pleased God (John 8:28–30). Do you think this would have been true if Jesus did not have a relationship with Him? I believe they had a very intimate relationship, and this is why the miraculous was seen in such great levels of manifestation in Jesus' life and ministry. Can you imagine what it would be like if we developed the same level of intimacy with God today?

Unfortunately, many so-called Spirit-filled Christians have settled for the mediocre. They accept far less than God ordained for them to walk in. I can only imagine how it must hurt Him to see this. He does not expect His children to settle for the status quo. God did not send Jesus to pay the price for our sin on the cross only to have us continue to live in bondage to sickness, poverty, or any other Satanic oppression. We are ordained for so much more. I believe the reason we are not experiencing it lies in our lack of intimacy with God. Paul's life and ministry was an example of dependence on the Holy Spirit built in relationship. He first encountered Jesus while traveling to Damascus on a mission to find and imprison Christians

(Acts 9). This encounter led to his conversion. He had been trained by some of the best theologians of his day and had risen to leadership in the Jewish religion. He would have been a prime candidate to thrust immediately into the ministry, but that was not God's plan. Paul spent three years in the deserts of Arabia before returning to Damascus and beginning his ministry.

I believe every Christian should aspire to follow Paul's example. We see an example of his complete dependence on Jesus in his life and ministry in 1 Corinthians 2:1–5:

> And I, brethren, when I came to you, did not come with excellence of speech or of wisdom declaring to you the testimony of God. For *I determined not to know anything among you except Jesus Christ and Him crucified.* I was with you in weakness, in fear, and in much trembling. And my speech and my preaching were not with persuasive words of human wisdom, but in demonstration of the Spirit and of power, that your faith should not be in the wisdom of men but in the power of God. (Emphasis added)

Paul could have leaned on his education and experience as a Pharisee, but he spent three years out of the spotlight before launching his ministry (Galatians 1:15–20). I believe this time was spent developing a relationship with the Holy Spirit. These verses show us his goal in ministry was to lead people into an encounter with the power of God. We should not look at Paul's ministry as one that set such a high bar that we will never reach it. God has given us the same Spirit, the same gospel, and the same measure of faith as He gave to Paul. It is time for us to stir up our hunger for the supernatural and make a commitment to pay whatever price is necessary to develop our relationship with the Spirit of God.

I do not believe you would be reading this book if you were willing to accept only a mediocre level of Christianity. In my experience, people who are content with just putting in their one or two hours a week at church are not seeking God for anything more. We all experience trials, and it is easy to fall into the trap of accepting things the way they are. Far too many of us are allowing ourselves to be satisfied with much less than the fullness of all God has planned for our lives. You are destined for greatness in the kingdom of God. The Holy Spirit is standing by to help you move into the measure of faith that is already in your spirit and start seeing God's power in demonstration. He is only waiting for your invitation.

Chapter 3

Activating the Power

So Jesus answered and said to them, "Have faith in God. For assuredly, I say to you, whoever says to this mountain, 'Be removed and be cast into the sea,' and does not doubt in his heart, but believes that those things he says will be done, he will have whatever he says. Therefore I say to you, whatever things you ask when you pray, believe that you receive them, and you will have them."

MARK 11:22–24

The original text of Mark 11:22 reads, "Have faith from God." There is a vast difference between having "faith in" versus having "faith from." I can have faith in someone or something with my natural human faith. For example, we exercise our faith every time we sit in a chair. We all have experience sitting in chairs and are confident they will hold our weight. There is a confident expectation in a chair's ability to hold us and not collapse when we sit down on it that is almost subconscious. This confidence is the result of personal experience sitting in chairs. I don't know of anyone who pauses to examine a chair before sitting on it.

I believe we all desire to live our lives to the fullest level possible. We cannot do this by just believing in God. I've met very few people who do not believe He exists. Most just do not know Him, and many have not accepted Jesus as their Lord as a result. They believe in Him but have no relationship with Him. It is not possible to move beyond mediocrity into a life characterized by manifestations of the Spirit if we are only believing in God. While that is a good starting point, we must press on into developing a personal relationship with Him. He has given us a measure of His faith that will begin to operate out of this relationship.

Increase Our Faith

I hope you are beginning to see that it is impossible to consistently walk in the miraculous by merely exercising your own natural human faith. Out of God's mercy, you may stumble across a miracle every now and again by accident. The good news is that He recognized the limitations of our faith, which is why He gave us the measure of His to live and operate in (Romans 12:3). He knew our faith would never measure up and provided us a measure of His faith to ensure we would always be able to access all that is available to us in Christ's redemptive work. I believe Paul was also aware of the limitations of our faith, based on his exhortation in Galatians 2:20 for his readers to live their lives by the faith of the Son of God. The verse reads "faith from the Son of God" in the original language, which is similar to what we saw in Mark 11:22. This is a better translation of the verse and is more in line with Hebrews 12:2, which tells us that Jesus is "the author and the finisher of our faith." The Greek word translated as "faith" in both Galatians 2:20 and Hebrews 12:2 is *pistis*, which we discussed in the previous chapter as always referring to a faith received as a gift from God.

Jesus' disciples recognized the limitations of their natural faith. They heard Him talk about forgiving people more than 400 times each day and asked Him to increase their faith so they could follow His instruction (Luke 17:1–5). The Lord responded, "If you have faith as a mustard seed, you can say to this mulberry tree, 'Be pulled up by the roots and be planted in the sea,' and it would obey you" (Luke 17:6). We most often interpret His statement as being focused on the size of the seed. The Holy Spirit challenged me to look more closely at the mustard seed one evening while sitting in a home Bible Study. I accepted His challenge and dedicated time over the next few months to studying the mustard seed.

Mustard plants have a central taproot that is the primary dominant root from which all others grow. I discovered that it will sometimes grow five to six feet deep into the soil before the first shoot appears above ground. The Holy Spirit asked me a question one evening while reading about the taproot. He asked, "Could it be that Jesus was referring to the depth of roots the Word is able to develop in your heart instead of the seed's size?" This was radically different from anything I had ever considered or heard taught. He led me to the parable of the sower in Mark 4, where we see Jesus describe the Word of God as a seed to be planted in the heart. Jesus described the operation of God's kingdom as being like a man casting seed into the ground and then resting (Mark 4:26–27). He knew we would be given a measure of God's faith and that it would be sufficient to produce a harvest of anything provided in His redemptive work. The size of the seed was not referenced at all in the parable of the sower.

Faith Is Not Governed by the Senses

The writer of Hebrews tells us that it is impossible to please God if we are not operating in faith (Hebrews 11:6). Once again, a form of the Greek word *pistis* is used. This is the same word translated as faith in Romans 1:17, Galatians 3:11, and Hebrews 10:38. All three of these verses repeat the phrase "the just shall live by faith." Paul uses the same word in 2 Corinthians 5:7, in which he tells us that we are to walk by faith and not by sight. In all these examples, the text is referring to a faith that cannot be accessed through self-effort. It is always received as a gift from God (Ephesians 2:8).

The word translated as "walk" in 2 Corinthians 5:7 is *peripateo*. It represents the way we conduct our lives. It is the same Greek word John used in 1 John 2:6, which tells us that we are to walk as Jesus walked. All aspects of our lives should be governed by the faith that has been given to us by God. We are meant to conduct our lives in the measure of faith given to us instead of by the input of our five physical senses. This made sense to me when I first saw it, but it did not help my understanding, as it was not clear that it meant we should conduct our lives as Jesus does. Over time, the Holy Spirit has shown me the verse is referencing how we respond to situations and circumstances. In other words, do we act as Jesus would if He were in our shoes, or do we react with things like unbelief, anxiety, or worry?

1 John 2:6 also tells us that it is those who "abide" in Jesus who walk as He walked. Abiding in Christ cannot happen if we are not spending time with Him in His Word. This is the fundamental principle of abiding. The word "abide" indicates a need to make our home in Christ Jesus. Doing so requires that we totally dedicate ourselves to the Word of God. We cannot respond to the situations of life as Jesus would if we are not completely focused on the Word. Too many of us have become distracted by the busyness of the world around us. As an example, I have had people ask for prayer to find deliverance from fear. Follow-up conversations with them revealed they were fixated on the daily news broadcasts. Their soul was filled with reports of death and destruction as a result, so they were responding to things happening in their lives from a position of fear. The Holy Spirit showed me I could pray for them, but deliverance would not come until they changed what was being fed into their souls.

Chapter 4

Faith Operates
from Our Spirit

For we walk by faith, not by sight.

2 CORINTHIANS 5:7

W e saw in the last chapter that the Greek word translated as "walk" in 2 Corinthians 5:7 is focused on the way our lives are conducted. The Holy Spirit helped me understand this is a reference to the way we react to the situations in our lives. In other words, the verse is telling us our behaviors should be governed by the Word of God. The Spirit reminded me of dinnertime when I was a child to help me understand this concept better. My family would usually try to eat dinner together each evening at a local restaurant, but we sometimes ate at home. I do not remember ever having to ask my parents to feed me dinner. It was supplied, so I would show up to the table with an expectation to be fed. There was no doubt in my mind that dinner would be available. I had faith in the provision provided by my parents.

God has given us a measure of His faith (Romans 12:3) and expects us to use it in every area of our lives. He also provided us with His Word to serve as our textbook on how to operate in His faith. We see in 2 Peter 1:3 that He has already provided for every area of our lives.

This provision is accessed through the "knowledge of Him," which can only be found in His Word. He sent the Holy Spirit to teach us and help us grow in our knowledge of Him. My point in bringing this up is to show that it is impossible to successfully operate in God's measure of faith without first developing a strong foundation in Scripture. I believe this was the point Jesus was trying to make in His reference to the mustard seed when He responded to the disciples' request for Him to increase their faith (Luke 17:6). He understood that the Word would serve as the foundation on which their lives would be built.

The idea of spending time meditating in God's Word each day is unfortunately a foreign concept for many Christians. The modern church seems to have built a culture focused on our ministers being tasked with studying Scripture and imparting God's truth to us. I hope you are beginning to see that this is not enough. Operating in faith requires us to become Word-minded, and this cannot happen if we are not spending time meditating in Scripture every day. Let's revisit my childhood dinner table to illustrate. I have a brother and sister. What do you think would have happened if I depended on them to eat and then tell me about the food that had been served? I probably would have become weak, sickly, and eventually starved, because my physical body needs to be fed. The same is true of our spirit. Many Christians are spiritually weak and struggling with faith because they are depending on their minister to partake of God's Word and then tell them what the Holy Spirit had served them. You cannot grow in faith if you are not sitting down to eat at the table prepared for you by your heavenly Father on a regular basis.

Faith from God Flows from Revelation Knowledge

One of the first verses the Holy Spirit took me to when He started to teach me about faith was Romans 3:27:

Where *is* boasting then? It is excluded. By what law? Of works? No, but by the law of faith.

This verse refers to "the law of faith." It tells us that the measure of faith given to us by God is governed by spiritual law. We have seen that faith is inseparable from the Word of God. This is a fundamental aspect of the law of faith. We have already seen that it is not possible to grow into His measure of faith without first committing to meditating in the Word of God every day. I have heard ministers refer to the importance of becoming "Word-inside" minded. This confused me when I was younger. Over time I've realized they were describing the need to allow ourselves to be governed only be the Word of God. Obviously it is not possible to eliminate all other input, as our society is filled with noise. We are inundated by things like background music at restaurants and at the mall. We also have phones that can instantly access the daily news headlines, our favorite television shows, or any other information we might want to look at. It is not surprising that Christians are distracted and living lives that look very similar to their unsaved neighbors. We tend to experience the same financial lack, depression, and sicknesses as unbelievers even though Jesus has provided us the means to overcome in every area of life through His redemptive work. The key to changing this and beginning to walk in God's full provision is to first make a firm decision to purposely protect ourselves by governing what is allowed to pass through our eyes and ears. In other words, we must become Word-inside minded!

Faith Is a Gift from God

We looked at Romans 10:17 in previous chapters. The Holy Spirit takes the incorruptible Word seeds (1 Peter 1:23) that are planted in our souls and uses them to "birth" the faith of God in our spirits. As we have seen, the Greek word translated as "hearing" in this verse represents our inner ear. This is our spiritual ear. Paul mentions the three parts of our being in 1 Thessalonians 5:23:

> And the very God of peace sanctify you wholly; and I pray God *your whole spirit and soul and body* be preserved blameless unto the coming of our Lord Jesus Christ. (Emphasis added)

Our soul consists of our mind, will, intellect, and emotions. We are first spirit. Our soul is the gateway between the spirit and the physical realm. When Paul wrote that we became a "new creature" in 2 Corinthians 5:17, he was speaking of our spirit. Our soul and physical body will not be fully changed until we either leave this world or we receive a glorified body when Jesus returns for the church. I mentioned in the previous chapter that Peter describes the Word of God as being an incorruptible seed (1 Peter 1:23). We plant that seed in our soul. James tells us that the Word will "save" our souls when it is able to become deeply rooted (James 1:21). The Holy Spirit will take that seed and use it to transmit God's measure of faith into our spirit.

Our relationship with God will always be through our spirit. It is our spirit that became a new creation when we were born again (2 Corinthians 5:17), and it is with the ear of our spirits we hear the voice of God. Developing a relationship with the Holy Spirit requires us to become more aware of the spiritual realm, which cannot happen without first giving constant and continuous attention to the Word of God. Once again, the Word is the foundation on which our entire spiritual life is built.

Paul tells us in Ephesians 2:8 that the measure of faith is a gift from God:

> For by grace you have been saved through faith, and that not of yourselves; *it is* the gift of God, not of works, lest anyone should boast.

I have heard ministers state grace is the gift Paul refers to in this verse. This was my understanding early in my ministry. Over time, I've realized he is telling us that the faith we used to receive salvation was a gift from God. It is His grace that enables us to receive it. We can do nothing to earn it or to cause it to grow in our spirit. The Holy Spirit breathed it into our spirit when we were still living in sin. He did this to ensure we had the ability to accept Jesus and experience the new birth. The same faith we used to receive Jesus as our Lord is the same faith He expects us to operate in throughout our Christian journey.

An Eternal Viewpoint

You will find that learning to discern between your natural faith and God's is one of the biggest challenges to operating in faith. The two are vastly different. We spoke briefly of the three parts of our being (spirit, soul, and body) in the last section. God's measure of faith operates from our spirit. Natural human faith operates from the soul. The soul acts as a gateway between our spirit and the physical realm. We will be dominated by our five physical senses if the Word of God is not being consistently planted in our souls. God's measure of faith will be blocked from flowing outward through our souls, and effectively lie in a dormant state. I picture a water pipe that has a clog blocking the flow of water when I think of the soul that has not been renewed by God's Word (Romans 12:2).

Paul describes the perspective of a person who allows the Word of God to become deeply rooted in their soul in 2 Corinthians 4:18:

> While we do not look at the things which are seen, but
> at the things which are not seen. For the things which
> are seen *are* temporary, but the things which are not seen
> *are* eternal.

I think of "things which are seen" as being things we can perceive with our five physical senses. Once again, faith is governed by the Word of God. Everything we can perceive in the natural realm around us is temporary. We are only on this planet for a short period of time. Our bodies will one day be cast aside when it is time for us to depart and enter eternity. The person governed by faith understands this. In a sense, we could say the person operating in God's measure of faith is governed by an eternal viewpoint.

The Eternally Fruitless Soul

We have already seen that God's measure of faith is governed by the law of faith (Romans 3:27). It operates out of our spirit but will be blocked if our soul becomes clogged. Jesus described this state in the parable of the sower when He spoke of the incorruptible seed that is planted in a soul that has become clogged with "the cares of this world, deceitfulness of riches, and the desires for other things" (Mark 4:19). He told His disciples that the Word of God cannot bear fruit if it is planted in a soul filled with these things. The original language describes this state as one that is eternally fruitless because the soul is not governed by God's Word or His faith. Can you imagine having to stand before God one day and listen to Him tell you that the reason His power was unable to flow in your life was because you allowed your soul to remain in this state? I believe Paul describes the difference between an eternally fruitful soul and a fruitless one in Romans 8:5–8:

For those who live according to the flesh set their minds on the things of the flesh, but those *who live* according to the Spirit, the things of the Spirit. For to be carnally minded *is* death, but to be spiritually minded *is* life and peace. Because the carnal mind *is* enmity against God; for it is not subject to the law of God, nor indeed can be. So then, those who are in the flesh cannot please God.

"Carnal" is a bit of an old-school word. In the context of this verse, it is referring to anything done apart from the measure of faith in our spirit. We could say Paul is describing the person who has not allowed their soul to be transformed by God's Word. In this sense, the carnal mind would be one that is governed by our self-nature, which is what I think of as the clogged soul. Paul tells us that a person living in this state is essentially an enemy of God and, as a result, will be unable to please God. We have already seen that it is not possible to please God without faith (Hebrews 11:6), so I feel it would be safe to say that the person operating from a carnal mindset will be unable to operate at any level in God's measure of faith. Any manifestation of the power of God in this person's life will be a result of God's mercy.

Chapter 5

Our Foundation
Is the Word of God

So then faith comes *by hearing,*
and hearing by the word of God.

ROMANS 10:17

The Greek word translated as "faith" in Romans 10:17 is *pis-tis*, which refers to a faith that is always received as a gift from God. This is a faith that cannot be generated through self-effort. It is completely dependent on God and His Word. I believe we have made the subject of faith much more complicated than it needs to be. There is no need for any person to jump through all sorts of hoops to get God's attention. He accepted us in Christ Jesus (Ephesians 1:6) and gave us a measure of His faith before we even turned to Him for salvation. Jesus told His disciples that our responsibility is to simply "cast" the incorruptible seed (His Word) into the ground of our souls and then to rest:

> And He said, "*The kingdom of God is as if a man should*
> *scatter seed on the ground, and should sleep by night and*
> *rise by day, and the seed should sprout and grow, he himself*
> *does not know how.* For the earth yields crops by itself: first

the blade, then the head, after that the full grain in the head. But when the grain ripens, immediately he puts in the sickle, because the harvest has come." (Mark 4:26–29, emphasis added)

We cast the seed into the ground of our souls and then rest. It is important to note that it is the earth that yields the crop once the seed is planted. Our job ends once the seed is in the ground. The seed will produce God's measure of faith on its own and does not need our help. There are no seven-step lists or any other natural resources generated by man that are needed for His faith to be imparted into our spirits.

The Inner Ear

Faith from God is received by hearing the Word of God. The Word is God's incorruptible seed that produces it. I have heard many messages over the years that focused on things like listening to audio Bibles, confessing Scripture, or listening to messages as tools to grow our faith. While it is important to do these things, Paul was not referring to just hearing with our physical ears. The Greek word translated as "hearing" in Romans 10:17 is *akoe*, which refers to hearing with our spiritual ear. We receive the measure of faith from God by becoming attuned to the spiritual realm and training ourselves to listen for His voice with our spiritual ears. This is done by spending time with the Word of God and in fellowship with the Holy Spirit. Unfortunately, far too many Christians are more immersed in the world around them than they are in their relationship with God. It will not be possible to tune into the voice of God if we are living only from our soul and five physical senses.

Paul tells us that those who live according to the Spirit of God will set their minds on the things of the Spirit (Romans 8:5). This is an interesting verse in the context of our study on the faith of the Son of God. It starts with a warning about walking "according to the flesh." The word "flesh" refers to those things originating from human effort. Do you remember me telling you earlier that faith received as a gift from God cannot be generated as a result of our efforts? Those who allow their lives to be governed by the Spirit of God will set their minds on Him by keeping their inner ear tuned to His voice. Paul used the word *rhema* in Romans 10:17 when he referenced the Word of God. This is a Greek word that describes the act of the Lord speaking His Word directly into our spirits. The Spirit of God is continuously speaking, but how many of us are listening with our inner ear to hear His voice? It all comes down to a matter of what we prioritize in our lives. Will we focus on the natural realm and the things that are important to us, or on the spiritual realm and the things that are important to God?

Faith Cannot Exist without the Word of God

We do not need to grow our faith. It was received as a gift from God (Ephesians 2:8). We can do nothing to increase or decrease it. Our role is simply to meditate in Scripture while simultaneously developing our relationship with the Holy Spirit. Our ability to operate in the measure of faith will increase as our relationship with Him grows. It really is that simple. I have discovered that operating in faith was only a challenge because I made it challenging. My focus was on what I could do to grow my faith instead of what I could do to grow my dependence on Him. There is a vast difference between dependence on self and dependence on God for the person whose goal is to operate in the measure of faith given to them by God.

I talk more about the relationship between the Word of God and the Holy Spirit in my book *The Holy Spirit and the Incorruptible Seed*.

For now, we simply need to know that the Spirit will be restricted in His ability to help us operate in the faith of the Son of God if we are not spending time meditating in the Word. He always operates in line with Scripture. As I have said previously, the Word of God is the foundation on which our entire Christian life is built.

Intimacy

Developing an intimate relationship with the Holy Spirit requires us to find a point of balance where we are not just pursuing the Word or the Spirit. It is not an either-or proposition. I like to picture a two-sided coin. On one side, people who pursue God's Word without the Holy Spirit's help usually end up suffering from a bad case of intellectualism that will be steeped in religious tradition. On the other side of the coin, people who only pursue the Spirit and neglect the Word tend to end up in fanaticism. I like to picture myself traveling on a road. Intellectualism is the ditch on one side and fanaticism the ditch on the other side. Our goal is to find a way to walk down the center line. The Holy Spirit will help us maintain this position if we ask for His help.

God has called and anointed me to teach His Word. You are also called to a specific task, career, or ministry. You might be called to be a plumber, electrician, or accountant. It will not be possible for any of us to fulfill the call on our lives without first developing an intimate relationship with the Word and the Spirit of God. He will impart wisdom and anoint us to accomplish any task if we look to Him and ask. We will find Him more than willing to help with every aspect of our lives. The problem is that most Christians seem to lack an awareness that He is with them. In most cases, the reason is a lack of teaching about Him and His ministry. In order to seek a person's assistance, you first need to recognize that they are available and eager to help.

The Revelation of Jesus Christ

We have seen that the Greek word translated as "hearing" in Romans 10:17 speaks to hearing with the ears of the spirit. Ministers have such busy schedules that many subscribe to services that provide them with weekly sermon messages. They do not have time to read the Word of God or pray. There are other ministers who spend so much time studying and polishing their messages that they deliver the sermon from their soul with no dependence on the Spirit. They have polished sermons that lead people into religious bondage and nothing more. The Holy Spirit warned me of the danger of this trap as my ministry was developing and I became more and more dependent on notes instead of His anointing. He showed me that I could not release the life of God while ministering from my soul. I believe this is the point Paul was trying to make in Galatians 1:11–12:

> But I make known to you, brethren, that the gospel which was preached by me is not according to man. For *I neither received it from man, nor was I taught it, but it came through the revelation of Jesus Christ.* (Emphasis added)

Paul was highly educated. He had been trained by some of the most renowned teachers of the day. If anyone could have preached from their education, it would have been him. He chose not to lean on his training, however, and instead ministered from a place of dependence on the Holy Spirit. We can follow Paul's example, but this will require us to develop a relationship with the Spirit. He is waiting for us. If you learn to bypass your soul and minister directly from your spirit, the Holy Spirit will take your words and use them to release the life of God directly into the spirit of those you minister to, whether you are standing behind a pulpit or engaging in a one-on-one conversation.

Accessing God's Hidden Wisdom

The gospel that Paul received by revelation of Jesus Christ is described as the wisdom of God in 1 Corinthians 2:6–8:

> However, we speak wisdom among those who are mature, yet not the wisdom of this age, nor of the rulers of this age, who are coming to nothing. But *we speak the wisdom of God in a mystery, the hidden wisdom which God ordained before the ages for our glory*, which none of the rulers of this age knew; for had they known, they would not have crucified the Lord of glory. (Emphasis added)

A biblical age refers to a cycle of time ordained by God. We currently live in what some call the Age of Grace. The Bible often refers to it as the last days. Regardless of what we call it, God ordained for His wisdom to be revealed to us before even the first age began. Sin made it inaccessible, though. Jesus eliminated the sin barrier that kept it hidden, and now, through Him, we can access it. Paul learned the secret to unlock it. His letters are filled with this wisdom. The Holy Spirit was sent to teach us how to access and operate in it. He does this as we spend time meditating in the Word of God. This wisdom enables us to operate in the measure of faith given to us by God.

The wisdom Paul refers to in 2 Corinthians 2:6–8 is the revelation of Jesus Christ that he spoke of in Galatians 1:11–12. It is the *rhema* knowledge we discussed while analyzing Romans 10:17. It is breathed directly into our spirits by the Holy Spirit as we spend time meditating in Scripture. This is the reason it was not available to those living under the old covenant. They were spiritually dead and could only interact with God on the soulish and physical levels. Wisdom received via *rhema* knowledge breathed into the human spirit was hidden from them because their spirits were dead and disconnected from God. People living before Jesus had no ability to connect with God spirit to spirit as we do today.

The Incorruptible Seed

The measure of faith cannot flourish where the Word of God has not first been planted. Peter described the Word as an incorruptible seed (1 Peter 1:23). Jesus also described it as a seed in His parable of the sower (Mark 4:15). The Holy Spirit took this truth and helped me understand the need to view each word in Scripture as a seed that operates like a container filled with the faith of God. He gave me a vision of a cupboard full of identical Tupperware containers filled with incorruptible faith seeds. I picture myself opening one of these containers and partaking of the contents each time I open my Bible to spend time meditating in it.

Jesus taught three parables to show how the Word operates in the kingdom of God just as a seed does in the natural realm. They are found in chapter 4 of Mark's Gospel. The first is the story of the sower. Jesus told His disciples it would provide them the key to understanding all His other teachings (Mark 4:13). As I've mentioned previously, the seed Jesus refers to in the parable is the Word of God (Mark 4:14), and the ground is our heart (Mark 4:15). God created our hearts with the ability to produce fruit from whatever seed is planted in it. We plant the seed and then need to give it time to germinate and develop roots in our hearts.

The seed must be left in the ground and given time to produce. Some people plant it and then begin questioning why it is isn't working after a day or two. They are digging the seed up with their words. If you did this with a natural seed, it would die and not produce fruit. Jesus describes three stages of growth in Mark 4:28 (KJV): "First the blade, then the ear, after that the full corn in the ear." There will be a temptation to become impatient and question the process. Those who yield will effectively dig up the seed they have planted, causing it to become dormant and unable to produce.

Let's look at salvation for an illustration of how the incorruptible seed operates. When you communicate the story of Jesus' saving work to someone who has never heard it, you are casting incorruptible seeds into their soul. These seeds will start to work immediately. The person can choose to reject it, but they cannot stop it from working. Over time, it will grow, and the person will begin to experience conviction. If they choose to yield to this, the seed will begin to develop roots. The Holy Spirit will use the seed to birth the measure of faith in that person's spirit, which, in turn, will give birth to belief in their soul. The person then has a choice to confess to Jesus as Lord and become born again, or refuse to act by making that confession. I have seen this process happen almost instantaneously, and I've also seen it operate over a period of years. I'm not completely sure why times are different, but based on what I've seen, I believe it has to do with the condition of the person's soul. Regardless of time frame though, God's incorruptible seed will work in the heart regardless of whether a person is saved or not.

Chapter 6

Faith Is a Gift from God

*"No one can come to Me unless the Father who sent Me
draws him; and I will raise him up at the last day."*

JOHN 6:44

W e closed the previous chapter with an illustration of the incorruptible seed being planted in the soul of an unsaved person. You need to understand that it is just not possible to believe in
God without first receiving His measure of faith. This cannot happen,
though, if the incorruptible seed of His Word has not been planted
in the soul. Paul references the process used by the Holy Spirit to get
the seed into the soul in Romans 10:14–15:

> How then shall they call on Him in whom they have not
> believed? And how shall they believe in Him of whom
> they have not heard? And how shall they hear without a
> preacher? And how shall they preach unless they are sent?

Everything comes back to the Word of God. Faith and belief cannot be received without it. The Word is God's incorruptible seed. The
seed must be planted and given time to grow. Unfortunately, we tend
to neglect it in our quest to find shortcuts. Paul understood this. We
see an example of this from his ministry in Acts 19:1–8. He arrived

in Ephesus and found twelve men who had followed John the Baptist. These men received Jesus and then received the Holy Spirit. Paul started to preach in the local synagogue but was rejected by the Jewish people. He did not try to force them to receive the Word of God or call for intercessory prayer or fasting as we probably would today. Instead, Paul withdrew to the school of Tyrannus with his twelve converts and spent the next two years planting the incorruptible seed:

> And he went into the synagogue and spoke boldly for three months, reasoning and persuading concerning the things of the kingdom of God. But when some were hardened and did not believe, but spoke evil of the Way before the multitude, he departed from them and withdrew the disciples, reasoning daily in the school of Tyrannus. And this continued for two years, so that all who dwelt in Asia heard the word of the Lord Jesus, both Jews and Greeks. (Acts 19:8–10)

Not much is known about Tyrannus. He may or may not have been a believer, and the room Paul used is thought by some to have been like a conference room we might rent today. We can reasonably assume that there were probably very few people in attendance beyond the twelve believers Paul met when he first arrived in Ephesus. He did not appear to be phased by this. Notice that he spent two years with that small group, but still "the word of the Lord Jesus" spread beyond the room where they met until "all who dwelt in Asia heard" the message Paul was preaching.

Have you ever heard anyone talk about the clothes that were taken from Paul and laid on the sick? We see this in Acts 19:11–12:

> Now God worked unusual miracles by the hands of Paul, so that even handkerchiefs or aprons were brought from

his body to the sick, and the diseases left them and the
evil spirits went out of them.

Many people have asked me why I feel we are not seeing the
miraculous in manifestation like the early church did in the book
of Acts. When I was younger, my answer would have been a lack of
prayer. But as I've spent time meditating on these verses in Acts 19,
the Holy Spirit has helped me see that the "unusual miracles" and
handkerchiefs did not occur until after the two years Paul spent sow-
ing the incorruptible seed at the school of Tyrannus. Paul understood the power of God's Word and the need to sow it. I believe we
do not see the miraculous in greater manifestation because we are
not reverencing the Word as the early church did. It is God's incorruptible seed that can produce a harvest of salvation, healing, and
fulfillment in our lives.

Do We Reverence the Word of God?

John tells us that Jesus was the Word of God (John 1:1–4,14). The
Word had to become a man in order to die as the final sacrifice for
humanity's sin. We could not save ourselves. Only a spotless man
able to live without sin could give His life to pay the requirements
of heaven's justice system. There was no other option for God than
to send His Word, Jesus, to the cross. Peter describes Jesus' sacrifice
in 1 Peter 3:18–22:

> For Christ also suffered once for sins, the just for the unjust,
> that He might bring us to God, being put to death in the
> flesh but made alive by the Spirit, by whom also He went
> and preached to the spirits in prison, who formerly were
> disobedient, when once the Divine longsuffering waited
> in the days of Noah, while *the* ark was being prepared, in

which a few, that is, eight souls, were saved through water. There is also an antitype which now saves us—baptism (not the removal of the filth of the flesh, but the answer of a good conscience toward God), through the resurrection of Jesus Christ, who has gone into heaven and is at the right hand of God, angels and authorities and powers having been made subject to Him.

It is only through Jesus that we can receive forgiveness for sin. He had to die and endure the horrors of hell to pay the penalty required by the court of heaven. Jesus obtained an eternal redemption (Hebrews 9:11–15) for us through His death, burial, and resurrection, but there was still a problem. Our natural human faith was not sufficient to receive the forgiveness He purchased. God sent Jesus to the cross on our behalf but then also had to enable us to receive His offer of salvation. Our condition was really that desperate. He had to find a way for us to receive it, so He made His very faith available. It comes to us through His Word as we see in Romans 10:14–15. There is not a single person who has ever come to the knowledge of salvation without first hearing the Word, receiving God's measure of faith, and then acting on that faith by confessing Jesus as their Lord.

Faith Is a Gift from God

God gave us a measure of His faith with no expectation of receiving anything in return while we were still living in sin. Paul tells us faith came to us as a gift offered through God's grace (Ephesians 2:8). Jesus' death on the cross was an expression of that grace. His crucifixion was the moment in time our heavenly Father showed His favor to humanity through the Lord's willingness to give Himself for our redemption. As mentioned previously, natural human faith is insufficient to accept God's offer of forgiveness, so He gave a measure of

His faith that enabled us to be saved from the sin nature we were all born into. However, it is impossible to receive this gift if we do not know it exists.

God expects His children to share the good news that He has provided a measure of His faith as a gift that is available to any who will receive it. He expects us to share this news with those who do not know Him. The gospel message is that He has provided everyone the means to escape from the prison of sin through Christ Jesus. The work is already finished, and God is only waiting for humanity to receive His gift. We are also expected to let people know that He offers them a measure of His faith that grants them the ability to receive the gift of salvation from sin and be set free to receive everything God has provided them in Christ.

Jesus told His disciples, "No one can come to Me unless the Father who sent Me draws him" (John 6:44). The Greek word translated as "draw" in this verse is *helkyo*, which refers to the power of attraction. I often think of a bug zapper as a perfect illustration of the gospel message when I read John 6:44. This is a device that attracts flying insects to its light and then zaps them when they make contact with its electrified coils. Every human being is born into sin with no way to escape. God sends His children to those still bound by sin with a message of hope that attracts them to Him. He provides a measure of His faith that enables them to accept His offer of salvation. I picture the sin nature being "zapped" the moment a person accepts the gift of salvation and is set free to enter the fullness of all God has provided them in Christ Jesus.

Demonstrating God's Power

Paul was a highly educated man. He could easily have thrilled his audiences with theologically sound sermons but chose another route that he described in 1 Corinthians 2:1–5:

> And I, brethren, when I came to you, did not come with
> excellence of speech or of wisdom declaring to you the
> testimony of God. For *I determined not to know anything*
> *among you except Jesus Christ and Him crucified.* I was with
> you in weakness, in fear, and in much trembling. And my
> speech and my preaching were not with persuasive words
> of human wisdom, but in demonstration of the Spirit and
> of power, that your faith should not be in the wisdom of
> men but in the power of God. (Emphasis added)

Paul had received the finest education available in the Jewish world but did not flaunt his knowledge. His message was simple— Jesus Christ and Him crucified. In contrast, I have heard so many ministers deliver sermons the average person would need a dictionary to even come close to understanding. There is a place for academic studies, but they must never replace the message of the cross.

Did you notice Paul spoke of demonstrations "of the Spirit and of power"? He ministered in partnership with the Holy Spirit. I encourage you to read through the book of Acts. Look for references to the Spirit. You will find that the early Christians had an awareness and respect for the Spirit of God that is largely missing today. In my experience, He is rarely mentioned in our services beyond just a passing mention.

I have said previously that the foundation on which our Christian lives are built is the Word of God. Without the assistance of the Holy Spirit, our time spent meditating in the Word will only lead to head knowledge, which I refer to as acquired knowledge. No person can develop a higher level of intimacy with the Word than the intimacy they have also found with the Holy Spirit. The reverse is also true. It is not possible to develop intimacy with the Spirit without also finding intimacy with the Word of God. Many people struggle in their Christian lives because they have not been taught this simple truth.

The Gospel and the Power

I believe every person desires to see miraculous demonstrations of God's power at some level. This is even true of people who do not know Him. Unbelievers may not understand it is His power they seek, but you can see evidence of their desire for the supernatural expressed in books, television shows, and movies. Paul's ministry included demonstrations "of the Spirit and power" that provided proof of his message. He even told his readers in Rome that the gospel message he preached was an expression of God's power leading people to salvation (Romans 1:16). I think of Mark 16:20, which tells us that "the Lord work[ed] with *them* and confirm[ed] the Word through the accompanying signs."

Do you remember the analogy I used in chapter 5 about the Tupperware containers? Let's revisit it in the context of our discussion about demonstrations of the power of God. Each of the containers is filled with God's incorruptible Word seed (1 Peter 1:23). In the context of Romans 1:16, we could say that each seed contains the power of God. Expanding on the analogy, we could say that we open the containers and partake of the incorruptible seeds while spending time meditating in the Word of God. Each seed contains God's power, so we are filling our souls with seeds that will release that power if they are allowed time to grow and germinate. There are far too many distractions in the world today. I believe Christians are not seeing greater manifestations of power because we have allowed our attention to be diverted from God's Word. This is the reason I emphasize the need to turn off our devices and spend focused time meditating in Scripture each day.

Paul understood the importance of the Word of God in the life of a Christian. He expressed his desire for his readers in Corinth to ground their faith in the power of God (1 Corinthians 2:1–5). *Pistis* is once again translated as "faith" in 1 Corinthians 2:5, pointing to the fact that it is a gift from God (Ephesians 2:8). I believe it is also important for us to note that the word translated as "in" ("… in the power of God") refers to the condition in which something operates from inside of something else. In context, Paul is speaking of the faith we receive from God. He is telling us that he desired for those who read his letter to operate from within the sphere of God's power (which he describes as the gospel in Romans 1:16) rather than within the sphere of their wisdom. In other words, his desire was for them to operate in the faith of God from a solid foundation built in God's Word.

Resting in the Growth Process

We looked at Jesus' comparison of faith to the mustard seed in chapter 3 and discussed the need to develop deep roots in the Word of God. Doing so requires us to first plant the incorruptible Word seed and then give it time to grow and become deeply rooted in our souls. Jesus described this process in the parable of the sower, which is found in Mark 4:26–29:

> And He said, "The kingdom of God is as if a man should scatter seed on the ground, and should sleep by night and rise by day, and the seed should sprout and grow, he himself does not know how. For the earth yields crops by itself: first the blade, then the head, after that the full grain in the head. But when the grain ripens, immediately he puts in the sickle, because the harvest has come."

Do you remember what we learned in Romans 10:14–15? These verses tell us that it is not possible to believe without first hearing the Word. Jesus told His disciples that the kingdom of God operates just like a farmer scattering seed on the ground. As mentioned earlier, the ground is the human heart. God sends people with revelation of His

Word to "scatter seed" in the ground by preaching the gospel message. He expects nothing else from us. We are not called to cause the seed to grow. Our job is to simply plant it, and then He expects us to rest while the Holy Spirit causes growth to occur.

Corruptible and Incorruptible Seeds

Did you notice that Jesus said the earth brings forth fruit of itself? The Greek word used in the verse is *automatos*, which is the word we most commonly translate into English as "automatic." Our hearts have been programmed by God to automatically cause the seed planted in them to grow. The Holy Spirit has brought me back to this truth many times over the years. As we have already seen, Peter spoke of corruptible and incorruptible seeds in 1 Peter 1:23:

> Having been born again, not of *corruptible* seed but *incorruptible*, through the word of God which lives and abides forever. (Emphasis added)

I believe this verse tells us that there are only two types of seeds that can be planted in the human heart. The news programs, sermons, and movies we consume will either plant corruptible or incorruptible seeds into our hearts. The heart is preprogrammed by God to cause the seeds to produce that we allow to be planted inside. Corruptible seeds will lead to a harvest of death that may manifest in the form of anxiety, sickness, or financial lack. Incorruptible seeds will lead to a harvest of life that may manifest as a healing, financial blessing, or deliverance. Far too many Christians are not paying enough attention to what they are allowing into their hearts. God has entrusted us with the responsibility to guard them and will not do it for us. He has given us His incorruptible seed, and the choice to plant it in our soul is ours alone to make.

We will never get to the point where all corruptible seeds are restricted from entering our hearts, but we can minimize how many pass through the gates of our eyes and ears by paying closer attention to our time spent watching television, looking at social media feeds, and listening to music. Mark 4:18–19 also describes the risks that distractions like these pose toward the incorruptible seeds that are able to enter our hearts:

> "Now these are the ones sown among thorns; they are the ones who hear the word, and the cares of this world, the deceitfulness of riches, and the desires for other things entering in choke the word, and it becomes unfruitful."

The cares of this world will choke the life out of the incorruptible seed, causing it to become unfruitful. A seed that has been choked is cut off from the life-support it needs to live. However, if the cares of this world, the deceitfulness of riches, and the desire for other things have the power to do this to the incorruptible seed, doesn't it make sense that the Word seed can have an equal effect on corruptible seeds? We can't keep corruptible seeds from being planted in our hearts, just as a farmer cannot stop weeds from being planted in his field. The thing we *can* do, though, is ensure that a greater volume of God's incorruptible seeds are planted in our hearts than corruptible seeds. Then the corruptible seed's life-support will be cut off, resulting in its death. I believe this is the point where we will begin to operate fully in the measure of faith given to us by God.

Chapter 7

Living by the Faith
of the Son of God

*I am crucified with Christ: nevertheless I live; yet not I, but Christ
liveth in me: and the life which I now live in the flesh I live by the
faith of the Son of God, who loved me, and gave himself for me.*

GALATIANS 2:20, kjv

God has given us the measure of His faith (Romans 12:3). We
have already spent some time discussing this truth. In my opinion, it is one that is not emphasized enough today. Far too often our
focus is on "our" faith. We have already seen that "our" faith will never
enable us to receive anything from God. You can follow any formula
or seven-step list to grow your faith, but it will still fall short. Natural human faith is weak, limited, and unable to access the provisions
God has provided in Christ's redemptive work. The measure of faith
given to us by God, on the other hand, is not limited.

Where our faith is weak, His faith is strong.

Where our faith is limited, His faith is limitless.

Where our faith is unable to access His provision, His faith unlocks
all that is provided to us in Christ's redemptive work.

God gave us His measure of faith (Romans 12:3) while we were
still sinners (Romans 5:8). We used it to receive His gift of salvation

by believing in Christ with our heart and confessing Jesus as our Lord (Romans 10:10). Many people do not realize it, but God did not give us the measure of His faith just to be born again. Paul tells us that we are expected to live our lives by it as well (Galatians 2:20). You can truly live life to the fullest by walking in the faith of the Son of God!

God's Measure of Faith

Our hearts received the incorruptible seed when we heard the gospel message (Romans 10:17) while still living in sin. We explored in chapter 6 how our hearts took that seed and immediately went to work. The Holy Spirit caused the seed to form roots in our souls, resulting in a release of the measure of faith into our spirits. A belief in Jesus grew from that faith, causing us to act and confess Jesus as our Lord and Savior. It was at that moment that the power of God was released into our spirits, causing them to be recreated (2 Corinthians 5:17). I believe this is what Jesus was describing in His conversation with Nicodemus when He said we must be born again (John 3:1–7).

Whether it be sickness, financial struggles, or anxiety, the Word of God is the incorruptible seed that can set us free. The seed's power is not limited to just these examples I've listed, though. Peter tells us that God has made provision for every need through the knowledge of Him who has called us (2 Peter 1:3). This knowledge is gained through personal experience with God's incorruptible seed. That seed must be planted in our hearts and nurtured through prayer. Our entire Christian lives are meant to follow the cycle of planting, growth, and harvest. Continuous planting leads to continuous growth, which, in turn, leads to a continuous harvest. We use the measure of faith through each step, and I believe this is the process Paul was referring to when he said the life we "live in the flesh" is to be lived "by the faith of the Son of God" (Galatians 2:20, KJV).

The Same Faith

Faith is found in the list of nine fruits that are present in the born-again human spirit (Galatians 5:22, KJV). As we have seen, the Holy Spirit used the incorruptible seed of God's Word to birth the measure of God's faith in our spirits. We used this faith to receive salvation and became new creatures in Christ Jesus (1 Corinthians 5:17). Our spirits were recreated at that moment, but God did not take back His measure of faith. His gifts are given and never taken back (Romans 11:29). Faith is one of His gifts. He gave it to us and now expects us to conduct every area of our lives using it.

In 2 Peter 1:1, Peter expresses that this is the same faith that he operated in. It is also the same faith Jesus and the early church walked in. You need to let that sink in. The same faith Jesus exercised when He raised Lazarus from the dead (John 11:38–44) has been given to you. This is the same faith Peter and John used to release a miracle into the body of the lame man at the Beautiful Gate in Jerusalem (Acts 3:1–10). I believe the reason we are not seeing the miraculous in greater manifestation is due to our lack of revelation regarding the measure of faith that is already in our hearts.

Calling Things That Be
Not as Though They Are

Since we've seen that God's gift of faith is far superior to our human faith, we should embrace His gift and do everything we can to exercise it. Our tongues are the primary tools we use to do this. The writer of Proverbs tells us that the power of life and death is in our tongues (Proverbs 18:21). We see an example of this in Romans 4:17 (KJV):

> (As it is written, I have made thee a father of many nations,) before him whom he believed, even God, *who quickeneth*

*the dead, and calleth those things which be not as though
they were.* (Emphasis added)

Notice the phrase "calleth those things which be not as though they
were." This is how God operates. It is also how He expects His children to operate. He is our heavenly Father, and it is only natural that
we, as His children, follow His example in our lives. This principle is
no different than a human child acting like their mommy or daddy.

So, how does this operate? Genesis 1:1–3 is a perfect example:

> In the beginning God created the heavens and the earth.
> The earth was without form, and void; and darkness was
> on the face of the deep. And the Spirit of God was hover-
> ing over the face of the waters. Then God said, "Let there
> be light"; and there was light.

God was surrounded with darkness. He said, "Let there be light."
The original language shows us He said, "Light come to be." There
was not light when He said this. That did not stop Him from calling for light.

Let's put this into practical terms. Your body may be afflicted with
a disease like cancer. Do you identify with the sickness or with the
Word of God? There are many scriptural promises you can choose
to stand on, such as 1 Peter 2:24, 3 John 1:2–4, or Psalm 107:20. For
our example, let's use the last verse, which tells us that God "sent His
Word and healed [us], and delivered [us] from [our] destructions."

Following God's example would mean confessing that He sent
Jesus, the living Word, and healed your body. One important point
that many miss when discussing these things is that we are not deny-
ing that the sickness is in our body. We also do not stop using natural medicine unless specifically instructed by the Holy Spirit to do

so. I have had God heal my body without using doctors, and I have had Him heal it through doctors. This is where relationship comes in. If you have invested the time into developing a relationship with Him, you will be positioned to hear His instructions immediately when hit with an unexpected attack like a symptom in your body. The problem is that we allow ourselves to become distracted by the noise of our society and are not able to clearly identify His voice in these times.

Faith in What Is Not Seen

Following God's instructions will require us to believe in things that cannot be perceived by our physical senses. There are people who argue that this is not possible, but it is. We cannot see heaven or hell but believe they exist. It is not possible to see our sins being removed, but we must believe they have in order to be born again. All these examples show us that it is possible to believe in things that cannot be seen. This is only possible, though, for the person operating in God's supernatural measure of faith.

We have looked at Romans 4:17 (KJV), which tells us that "God ... calleth those things which be not as though they were." The verse presents us with a picture of how God's faith operates. It is vastly different from our natural human faith, which can only believe in what it can see, taste, hear, smell, or feel. In other words, our faith is limited to the input of our five physical senses. God's faith is not constrained by this limitation and is therefore able to look into the spiritual realm where we access all that has been provided for us in Christ's redemptive work.

The reference to "things which be not" is a reference to things that can be perceived by our physical senses. Operating in the faith of God does not mean we deny the existence of the sickness, anxiety, or other hardships that we may experience in the natural realm.

Instead, it means looking into the mirror of God's Word and declaring the provision that has already been provided in Christ Jesus.

Romans 4:17 is specifically speaking of the time when God supernaturally blessed Abram and Sarai with a child. Abram was 100 years old and Sarai was 91 when this happened. God told them He was going to do this the year before the promised child was born. He also changed Abram's name to Abraham, which means "the father of a multitude." Romans 4:17 tells us that He did this because He was calling the thing that did not yet exist in the natural realm as if it had already manifested. God has given every person access to a measure of His faith and expects us to follow His example.

I have been blessed to sit under many renowned faith teachers and have probably listened to hundreds of messages focused on faith. It still surprises me how much I struggled to understand faith with this foundation. The Holy Spirit has helped me understand that my troubles with the faith message stemmed from the lack of separation between my faith and the measure of faith. Most of the messages I've heard mixed the two and left myself, and many others I've met, confused as a result.

As we move forward in our study, it is important to keep in mind that there is not a clear line of demarcation between our faith and God's. We do not have to choose one over the other. You will always need to exercise your natural faith for things like sitting in a chair, riding in a car, or flying in an airplane. These are natural events that do not require supernatural intervention to occur. We use God's faith to appropriate His provision and miraculous power. There will always be a need to find balance, and that is where our relationship with the Holy Spirit becomes vital. He will guide each step of our journey and help us always stay in the center of the road.

Chapter 8

Distractions Prevent Us from Operating in Faith

Jesus said to him, "Thomas, because you have seen Me, you have believed. Blessed are those who have not seen and yet have believed."

JOHN 20:29

I used to work with a local cable company, performing contract service installations. It was always interesting to see how people reacted when a technical issued caused us to delay their service. In most cases, we were able to come back the next day. Twenty-four hours without cable, phone, and internet does not seem like a terrible thing, does it? Surprisingly, we left a lot of our customers in tears at the thought of not being able to watch their favorite television program, movie, newscast, or sporting event.

My contract ended more than fifteen years ago. We have a lot more distractions today than anyone could have imagined back then. I mention the cable contract to illustrate how outwardly focused we have become. I have also previously mentioned the relationship the Holy Spirit desires to have with us. In the natural realm, relationships with other people require a commitment of time and effort in order to succeed. Our relationship with the Spirit is no different. He desires to spend time with us but will not force Himself into our lives.

65

The distractions of life pull our attention away from Him, and as a result, many Christians today know about Him but do not know Him.

The Holy Spirit loves to spend time with us but will never demand that we spend time with Him. I believe the distractions of this world have become much more appealing to many Christians than spending time with the Holy Spirit. I have said many times in previous chapters that the Word of God is the foundation from which our ability to operate in God's faith flows. Your intimacy with the Word will be a direct reflection of your relationship with the Spirit of God. It is impossible to become intimately familiar with one and not the other.

The distractions of our world have made us far too dependent on our five physical senses. I recently took part in a meeting at our local church in which participants stepped away from their day-to-day responsibilities to seek God for forty-eight hours. We had an activity on the second day that required everyone to sit still for twenty minutes with no music, phones, televisions, or any other distractions. It amazed me to see how difficult this exercise was for most people in the room. One of my instructors used to have us sit in chairs with our hands folded in our laps and spend time praying. We were not allowed to stand, walk, or do anything else but sit still. This was an extremely difficult task, but it was also one of the most valuable, as it taught me to look beyond the input of my physical senses to the Holy Spirit.

Faith and the Five Physical Senses

God's measure of faith has been deposited in the spirit of every Christian. Activating it requires us to learn to live from the spiritual realm. The distractions we have been discussing force our attention outward. This reminds me of a phrase the Holy Spirit once shared with me. He said, "Your dominant point of meditation is the determining factor for the dominant manifestations occurring in your life." Let's apply this principle to the daily news headlines as an example. If we are spending more time meditating on the news, our souls will be full of corruptible seeds that will create a clog capable of blocking the life of God from flowing outward from our spirits. These seeds will eventually create a harvest of fear, anxiety, and worry if we allow them to grow and germinate. God's measure of faith will effectively be forced into a dormant state as a result. The Christian who allows their soul to be filled with corruptible seeds from the world will be unable to experience any level of intimacy with either the Spirit or the Word because their five physical senses will be governing their lives.

In a sense, learning to look inward to the Spirit is like paddling a canoe upstream. Like the current of the stream, society is flowing in a single direction away from God. Turning our spiritual canoe to move in the opposite direction will meet resistance. The enemy will use our friends, family, and even church activities to distract us from spending time alone with the Word and the five physical senses if we let him. It will require a level of discipline that most Christians don't seem willing to adopt in order to successfully pursue the Word and the Spirit.

I believe you are different than the majority and will make the commitment to discipline yourself. Jesus spoke of the well of living water during His conversation with the Samaritan women in John 4:13–14. In the context of the canoe analogy, a river flows outward from its source. Our source is Jesus. Your commitment to building your relationship with the Word and the Spirit will cause you to turn toward the well containing this living water. It will require you to turn the canoe of your life around and begin paddling against the current the world is following. At first, it will seem like all the forces of hell are pushing against you, but if you keep paddling, you will push through the resistance and see the measure of faith begin to operate in your life.

An Enviable Position

Jesus told Thomas that those who learn to believe without any corresponding physical evidence will be blessed. The Greek word translated as "blessed" in this verse refers to a believer in an enviable position. In other words, the person who can believe the Word despite what their body or society is telling them is in a much better position than the person who is governed by the input of their five physical senses.

I can sense that there will be some who read these word and question why God would allow one person to be in an enviable position over another. The answer to this is simple: He does not. We all are given the same measure of faith, but it is our choice to operate in it or not. God will never force us to do anything.

I have found that operating in the miraculous is not as difficult as many think. It requires a level of commitment and a high level of discipline to maintain. However, the people who do this and surrender themselves completely to the Holy Spirit will be the ones who experience the miraculous power of God.

I believe a lot of confusion around the miraculous is due to a lack of balanced teaching. We talk about the miraculous, need for revival, and manifestations of the Spirit, but how many times have you heard a message about learning to look inward to the Spirit or about avoiding distractions to sit quietly with Him? In my experience, these types of messages are few and far between. We gravitate toward seeking an experience that touches our physical being instead of pursuing relationship with God.

What Are We Looking At?

Satan has unfortunately been very successful in his efforts to draw our attention away from the spiritual realm. It almost seems as if his tactics are endless, but they are not. I have found distraction to be one of his most successful tactics, which is the reason I've mentioned it so many times. We have things like video games, social media accounts, and our televisions screaming for our attention. It is an unfortunate fact that far too many Christians have allowed themselves to become much more intimate with these things than with the Word of God and the Holy Spirit. The bottom line is that you will never operate effectively in the measure of faith without first developing your relationship with God. All relationships require a commitment of time.

Ignorance of the Spiritual Realm

Satan has sadly been far too effective in His efforts to draw our attention outward to what is happening in the natural realm. In my opinion, this has been largely due to our ignorance of the spiritual realm. We serve God, but how many of us have invested any time in developing a relationship with Him? I have met a lot of people who would argue that they have done this, but their life tells a different story. I believe that the fundamental reason for this is that many of those standing in the pulpit are filling a job and not a calling. If the person at the top does not have a relationship with the Holy Spirit, how can those in their congregations have one? It is not possible to lead a person to a place we have never gone ourselves in the natural or spiritual realm.

We often quote 1 Corinthians 12:1 in the context of spiritual gifts. In it, Paul writes, "Now concerning spiritual *gifts*, brethren, I do not want you to be ignorant." There is a problem, though, with the way this has been translated, because "gifts" is not in the original language. The Greek word translated as "spiritual" is *pneumatikos*, which refers to the realm of the spirit, where the Holy Spirit imparts faith and reveals Christ to us. I believe Paul was expressing a desire for his readers to become more inwardly focused. He recognized that everything we receive from God, including His measure of faith, flows outward from the spirit. This fits into our conversation because the distractions of life can turn your attention outward to the natural realm. As I said before, I don't believe you will let that happen, and I pray the Holy Spirit will open your spiritual eyes and help you become much more aware of His presence within.

Chapter 9

Believe without Physical Evidence

Now when Jesus had entered Capernaum, a centurion came to Him, pleading with Him, saying, "Lord, my servant is lying at home paralyzed, dreadfully tormented." And Jesus said to him, "I will come and heal him." The centurion answered and said, "Lord, I am not worthy that You should come under my roof. But only speak a word, and my servant will be healed. For I also am a man under authority, having soldiers under me. And I say to this one, 'Go,' and he goes; and to another, 'Come,' and he comes; and to my servant, 'Do this,' and he does it." When Jesus heard it, He marveled, and said to those who followed, "Assuredly, I say to you, I have not found such great faith, not even in Israel! And I say to you that many will come from east and west, and sit down with Abraham, Isaac, and Jacob in the kingdom of heaven. But the sons of the kingdom will be cast out into outer darkness. There will be weeping and gnashing of teeth." Then Jesus said to the centurion, "Go your way; and as you have believed, so let it be done for you." And his servant was healed that same hour.

MATTHEW 8:5–13

A Roman centurion approached Jesus for his servant's healing. He was not a Jew, but still exercised faith in a way that is a perfect illustration of Hebrews 11:1, which tells us that "faith is the substance of things hoped for and the evidence of things not seen." The original Greek translation of this verse indicates that "faith is the assurance of things hoped for and the conviction of the things not seen." I know you might be wondering how this verse correlates to the Roman centurion. He approached Jesus with a conviction that if the Lord would just speak a word, healing power would be released in his servant's body. His faith had developed to the point that He only needed the Word of God as evidence that the healing was complete. He did not need Jesus to follow Him home to lay hands on the servant or anoint him. This amazed Jesus, and He turned to His followers and said, "Assuredly, I say to you, I have not found such great faith, not even in Israel!" (Matthew 8:10).

The Word of God Is Sufficient

The Roman centurion was not Jewish, and he lived before the cross. It seems he would not have had access to God's measure of faith as we do today. I used to think this way, but then I noticed that Matthew used the Greek word *pistis* to describe the centurion's faith. We have seen elsewhere that this word always refers to a faith that originates with God. If an unbelieving centurion was able to exercise God's gift of faith to the level of receiving a miracle for his servant, how much more should we be seeing manifestations of power today when we exercise it? Jesus told the centurion that he would receive according to his belief, which only required a word from Jesus (Matthew 8:13). The Word of God was sufficient, and he needed nothing else from the Lord.

I have had many people ask me to pray for their healing over the years. Most act as if they are believing in God, but the majority will start immediately looking for a physical change in their body after I pray for them. The Word of God is not enough for them. This reminds me of a situation that occurred just after Jesus appeared for the first time to His disciples after being resurrected. Thomas was not with them and refused to believe the Lord was alive without some form of accompanying proof (John 20:24–25). He chose to cling to the things his five physical senses could interact with. By contrast, the centurion was satisfied with just a word from Jesus. In every situation, you and I have a choice to make. Will we follow Thomas or the centurion's example? Jesus rebuked Thomas but marveled at the Roman centurion. How do you think He is responding to your faith today?

A Commitment to the Word of God

You will not become a master of the measure of faith overnight. There will be failures and missteps that will need to be corrected. The good news is that you are not alone on this journey. Jesus sent the Holy Spirit to be with you. Every child of God should be led by Him in every area of life (Romans 8:14). He desires to work with us but will not force Himself on us. You will find there are some people who always receive His help more often than others do. This used to bother me, and I asked Him about it. It seemed He played favorites, but the Spirit assured me He does not. The reason some people receive more help from Him than others is simply because they have asked Him to help them.

You are the sole decision-maker when it comes to the level you reach regarding operating in the measure of faith. God has given you His Word and His Spirit, but you must make a commitment to spend time each day with both. It is our lack of relationship with these two ingredients that causes us to struggle so much with the operation of faith. I have found that the more time I commit to the Word and the Spirit, the more effortlessly the measure of faith works in my life.

The Word of God must become the final authority in our lives to activate the measure of faith. If we will shut off everything else to spend focused time with it each day, we will be able to stand with a confident expectation of receiving the full manifestation of God's promises, regardless of any contrary input from our soul or five physical senses.

Looking Beyond What Is
Perceived by Our Physical Senses

I have heard some people teaching the faith message encourage others to deny what is happening in the natural realm. They say things like, "Deny your symptoms," "Deny your unpaid bills," or "Deny your sin." Walking by faith will never require us to deny what is happening in the physical realm. Hebrews 11:1 tells us that "faith is the substance of things hoped for and the evidence of things not seen." God's measure of faith grows from the incorruptible seed of His Word. No physical evidence is necessary to recognize His provision. The centurion who approached Jesus operated in God's faith. He only needed a word from Jesus to know his servant had been healed and did not need any physical evidence to show the healing had occurred.

The person operating in faith makes a conscious decision to consider the Word of God over any situation occurring in their life. If their body is saying cancer, they will respond with a verse like 1 Peter 2:24, fully confident the Word will push the cancer out of their bodies. Their confidence is built on the Word of God and nothing else. It takes an unbreakable determination to commit to this path. Satan will do everything he can to stop us from moving into a totally Word-dominated life.

The Need for Wisdom

Paul tells us we can choose to look at the unseen by looking into the Word of God. We do this by looking at God's Word instead of any symptoms that may exist in our bodies. I must caution you, though, that it takes time for the Word to become deeply rooted in your soul. You must use wisdom and maintain a very close relationship with the Spirit of God. He will guide you, but only if you have invited Him to do so and are listening to His direction.

I have had people ask me if walking by faith means disregarding all medical treatments. There is a need for wisdom in the faith walk. We live in a fallen world and will experience physical symptoms in our bodies. You must not allow yourself to be condemned if this happens to you. Doctors and medical treatments should be looked at as an aid to use while developing ourselves in faith—in the same way a person with a broken leg would use a crutch. If we place our focus on the Word of God, our faith will grow, and the Holy Spirit will tell us when we are ready to stop taking any prescribed medicine or discontinue medical care. In most cases, I have observed that He will usually lead us to finish the full course of medicine with an expectation that it will not be needed the next time Satan attacks us with the same symptoms.

Our Soul Is the Battleground

I have heard ministers say that developing in faith is an easy process, but they are wrong. It requires an unshakable commitment to the Word of God. At times, it will seem as if Satan has pulled out his entire arsenal to keep you from succeeding. His primary weapon will be thoughts focused on causing you to doubt God's Word. Paul tells us in 2 Corinthians 10:3–6 that spiritual warfare is fought in our thoughts:

> For though we walk in the flesh, we do not war according to the flesh. For the weapons of our warfare are not carnal but mighty in God for pulling down strongholds, casting down arguments and every high thing that exalts itself against the knowledge of God, bringing every thought into captivity to the obedience of Christ, and being ready to punish all disobedience when your obedience is fulfilled.

I have heard a lot of teaching about strongholds over the years. Most have focused incorrectly on things like strongholds over a city or region. In context, Paul used the word to describe arguments and any other thought that opposed the knowledge of God. This is validated by the Greek word *ochuroma*, which is translated as "stronghold" in 2 Corinthians 10:4. The word is used by Paul to describe false arguments in which a person will seek an escape.

Strongholds and a Miracle Healing

We have used healing for illustration. A stronghold in this area can be illustrated by the healing of a young lady almost thirty years ago. Beth was the pianist for her church. She had suffered a debilitating disease as a young child and needed two crutches that attached at her wrists to walk. The healing anointing manifested one evening, and Beth was miraculously healed. We praised the Lord as she ran, jumped, and danced without her crutches for the first time!

My heart sank the next night to see Beth arrive to service with her crutches. She hobbled into service and sat at the piano bench as if the miracle did not take place. This did not make sense to me. Beth had obviously received a miracle, and I struggled to understand how she ended up in the same condition less than twenty-four hours later.

I spent many hours discussing Beth with the Holy Spirit. He led me to 2 Corinthians 10:4 and spent some time talking to me about strongholds. They will usually manifest in our souls as a picture in our imagination. The pastor discovered Beth had an image of herself as the crippled girl. She had been afflicted by her condition for so long that it created this stronghold in her soul. Her parents were not at service when the miracle occurred, but they had similar strongholds in their souls. Beth returned home, and her mother almost panicked at the sight of her walking without the crutches. She convinced Beth to keep them nearby in case the miracle "failed." Beth reverted to the dominant image in her soul and ended up back in her crippled condition.

How Do You See Yourself?

Beth had not been taught about faith or healing. Paul talks about the need to renew our minds with the Word of God (Romans 12:2). This basically means reprogramming our souls to produce images based on God's promises rather than symptoms that may be occurring in our souls or bodies. If Beth had been attending a church that taught these things, her dominant image would have been of "Beth the healed girl." She may or may not have needed the miracle, but she would not have reverted to her crippled condition if she did.

Your eyes and ears are the gateways to your soul. You are the gatekeeper, and your dominant internal image in your soul is determined by what you allow to be sown into it. Satan tempts us with any number of distractions to keep us from looking consistently at the Word of God. He would much rather have us sit mindlessly in front of the television for hours on end than sit quietly with Scripture.

The critical factor in whether we operate successfully in the measure of faith or continue to struggle in our faith walk is the strongholds we allow to be built in our souls. Paul portrays them negatively in 2 Corinthians 10:4. While it is true that strongholds that oppose the Word of God can be built in our soul, I believe it is also possible to meditate on His promises to the point that they develop positive strongholds that oppose anything contrary to the Word. The decision for us, then, is whether we allow the strongholds inside of our souls to be formed by the promises of God, society, or our physical conditions. We are the sole decision-maker about what our dominant point of focus will be. The strongholds in our souls are a direct result of this decision. They will either be Word-based or world-based. Which direction are you going to choose?

Chapter 10

The Role of Hope in Receiving God's Promises

Now faith is the substance of things hoped for, the evidence of things not seen.

HEBREWS 11:1

I struggled with understanding the measure of faith until I started to make time to fellowship with the Holy Spirit. He has really helped me understand how God's faith works and how to grow into it. You will find Him waiting to do the same for you. He is very patient and will work with us at our pace and never pressure us. There have been times when I allowed myself to become busy and neglected spending time with Him as a result. I always found Him waiting, though, when I turned back and shut everything off to focus on our time together.

Early in our journey together, the Spirit showed me that a lot of the troubles I had experienced with faith resulted from my bypassing the subject of hope. This was an area I had not previously thought much about. The Spirit helped me see from Scripture that faith cannot work without hope and hope cannot work without faith. This is the reason Hebrews 11:1 mentions hope. Faith and hope work hand in hand. I served in the US Navy and spent time at the firing range while in boot camp. In a sense, hope is like the targets we shot at, and faith is like a gun. We could say that hope gives aim to our faith. Until I made this connection, Satan used my ignorance in this area to sow confusion in my soul.

The Hope of His Calling

Paul penned a prayer in Ephesians 1:15–21 that I have prayed multiple times for myself, my family, and many others over the years:

> Therefore I also, after I heard of your faith in the Lord Jesus and your love for all the saints, do not cease to give thanks for you, making mention of you in my prayers: that the God of our Lord Jesus Christ, the Father of glory, may give to you the spirit of wisdom and revelation in the knowledge of Him, the eyes of your understanding being enlightened; that you may know what is the hope of His calling, what are the riches of the glory of His inheritance in the saints, and what *is* the exceeding greatness of His power toward us who believe, according to the working of His mighty power which He worked in Christ when He raised Him from the dead and seated *Him* at His right hand in the *heavenly* places, far above all principality and power and might and dominion, and every name that is named, not only in this age but also in that which is to come.

Paul lists three specific areas in which he desired his readers to develop knowledge: 1) the hope of God's calling, 2) the riches of the glory of His inheritance in the saints, and 3) the exceeding greatness of His power toward us who believe. It surprised me to see that Paul did not include faith in this list.

In the first item listed in the Ephesians prayer—the hope of our calling—the word "calling" is translated from the Greek word *klesis*, which refers to God's invitation to receive His gift of salvation and all the blessings associated with it. In other words, hope will generate an expectation within our heart that we will receive all God has provided in salvation.

I struggled with understanding faith because my spiritual eyes had not been opened to the power of hope. There was no revelation in my heart of the relationship between faith and hope. God's measure of faith had been given to me, and I had used it to receive Jesus, but I did not understand how to use it in my Christian journey to accomplish the plan of God. The Holy Spirit helped me in this area by leading me to 1 Corinthians 13:13, which reads, "And now abide faith, hope, love, these three; but the greatest of these *is* love." Faith, hope, and love form the foundation of our Christian lives. It was God's love for humanity that resulted in Jesus being sent to the cross for our redemption (John 3:16). Love opened the door for us to be saved, hope created a desire to be saved, and faith led us to the confession of Jesus as Lord.

What Is Hope?

I saw the importance of hope and then asked the Spirit how to develop it in my heart. He led me to Romans 8:23–24:

> Not only *that*, but we also who have the firstfruits of the Spirit, even we ourselves groan within ourselves, eagerly waiting for the adoption, the redemption of our body. For we were saved in this hope, but hope that is seen is not hope; for why does one still hope for what he sees?

Notice the verse tells us that "we were saved in this hope" regarding "the redemption of our body." I spoke earlier of the need to learn how faith enables us to look beyond the things that are perceived with our physical senses. Paul tells us in these verses that hope is always focused on those things that are not "seen." The Greek word translated as "seen" in verse 24 is *blepo*, which refers to the ability to see something as accomplished in the physical using only our spiritual perception. In the context of salvation, hope enables us to see the promised redemption of our physical bodies using only the eyes of our spirit. Hope set the goal, and faith received the promise of salvation. This was the point at which God rescued us from the penalty and power of sin to set us on the road toward the redemption of our physical bodies that will occur when Jesus returns for His church. Hope enables us to "see" that as an accomplished fact even though it has not yet happened.

As I started to recognize how hope was essential to my ability to operate in the measure of faith, it occurred to me that I did not really understand hope. I had not heard many ministers teach on this subject, which still surprises me. I cannot point fingers, though, because hope was not a subject I had taught on up to that point either. Without realizing it, I, too, had fallen into the trap of pursuing faith as the answer to all of life's problems. However, hope does not work in a vacuum, so there was a lot more for me to learn before I started seeing results in my faith walk.

The Relationship between Hope and Desire

It is impossible to receive anything from God without first hoping for it. In Romans 8:23–24 we saw the connection between hope and our salvation. These verses showed us that hope is always looking forward to receiving what we are expecting to receive from God. The dictionary defines hope as a desire coupled with expectation or fulfillment. This is a good starting point, but we also need to look at how the

Word of God defines hope. Let's consider Proverbs 13:12, which reads, "Hope deferred makes the heart sick, but *when* the desire comes, *it is* a tree of life." I have heard the first part of this verse quoted many times over the years. The Holy Spirit asked me to look at the whole verse one morning in service when our pastor referenced it. He had just started teaching me about hope, and I truthfully had never paid much attention to the second half of the verse. Taken together, the two halves express that hope and desire are inseparable. In a sense, we could say that hope is desire and desire is hope. Both look forward to receiving the things that cannot be perceived with our physical senses.

Chapter 11

Faith Is a Gift to Be Used in This Life

Now faith is the substance of things hoped for, the evidence of things not seen.

HEBREWS 11:1

I was saved in what some would call an old-line Pentecostal church. The name on the door does not matter. What is relevant is that the church believed in the Holy Spirit but rarely talked about faith. God called me to the ministry and led me to attend a Bible school that was known for being at the forefront of what some would call "the faith movement." I am extremely thankful for the education I received, as it laid the foundation for my ministry. Unfortunately, it also led me to struggle for many years as I attempted to understand faith and how to activate the measure I had been given in my life. My lack of understanding regarding the connection between faith and hope was largely to blame.

Faith Is Always Now

I had to overcome a lot of incorrect perceptions when I first started learning about the connection between hope and faith. For instance, I thought faith was only pertinent to our present life, and hope was only pertinent to our future life with Christ. It was almost as if I did not think God would give me access to the benefits provided in Christ's redemptive work until this life ended. My family had attended a church while I was growing up that believed God used the trials and tribulations of life to keep His children humble. The religious traditions they filled my head with became a stronghold in my soul that literally robbed me from experiencing the joy of my salvation.

I sat under some of the best faith teachers alive while in Bible school. Unfortunately, their teaching was unable to enter my soul and take root because of the religious stronghold from my childhood. When I think back on those times, I'm reminded of Jesus' words in Mark 7:13: "…making the word of God of no effect through your tradition which you have handed down." Things did not begin to change for me until I finally hit rock bottom due to several personal tragedies that occurred in my life. It was at the point where I was completely broken that I finally immersed myself in the Word and began to spend hours each day alone with the Holy Spirit discussing the things I was reading in Scripture. He took me to 2 Corinthians 10:5 and showed me that freedom would not come until I first overthrew that stronghold by taking it captive with the Word of God. This required me to fill my soul with the incorruptible Word seed to the point where there was no longer any room for corruptible seeds to take root. You can do the same thing I did. God does not play favorites. He wants all His children to enjoy the benefits of their salvation in this life. Peter tells us He has made provision for every need we will have in this life (2 Peter 1:3).

Breaking Free from Religious Tradition

Many people sit in church week after week who are just as limited as I was by strongholds built in their souls by religious tradition. They love God and desire to please Him but have never been exposed to truth. Their ministers offer hope only for an eternal destination, and so they live with no expectancy of receiving anything more from God than the everyday struggles that this world offers. They suffer with the same issues as their unsaved neighbors and are starving for truth that can only be found in the Word of God.

I have heard many ministers in so-called "faith churches" make fun of these people. I fell into this trap and became very critical of anyone outside of my group. Thankfully, the Holy Spirit corrected me. He helped me recognize that people attend dead churches that preach religious traditions out of their desire to serve God. They know nothing else and are stuck in an endless cycle of defeat and failure. I've spent many hours discussing these things with the Holy Spirit. He has shown me that even the churches we perceive as being alive and healthy also have traditions that are sucking the life out of good-hearted Christians. The name on the church sign does not matter. We all have strongholds of doubt and unbelief in our souls that can only be torn down by the Word of God. Hope cannot be activated until this happens.

Faith Is the Victory

We see in 1 John 5:4 that we are to overcome the world using faith that is a gift from God. The original translation of this verse is interesting, as it reads, "Everyone having been born of God overcomes the world and *this is the victory—having overcome the world the faith [pistis]*." God has given us a measure of His faith that has already overcome the world. Christians use it to overcome their world and are doing so from a place of victory already won by Christ Jesus in His redemptive work. This is an amazing perspective that we need to embrace. Jesus won the victory using the faith of God, opened the door to salvation, and then gave us access to operate in the same faith He used to already overcome!

I recognize that these truths may be new to you. You might even disagree with me that it is possible to experience victory over every situation in this life. That is fine. I am not asking you to believe me or any other minister. My recommendation is to take time to sit quietly with the Holy Spirit. Ask Him to show you the truth from Scripture. You will find Him eagerly waiting to do so. The journey into truth begins by acknowledging the Spirit and developing a relationship with Him. Jesus told His disciples that one aspect of the Holy Spirit's ministry is to guide us into all truth (John 16:13). He will teach you how to develop in hope, impart vision into your spirit, and guide you into the measure of faith given to you be God. Spontaneous victories will follow!

Faith Is Not Future Tense

Jesus tells us in Mark 7:13 that our traditions will render the Word of God powerless in our lives. These traditions usually manifest within our church or denomination in the form of false teachings. In my experience, problematic traditions always emphasize the future. For instance, ministers often talk about the promises of God being manifested one day in the future. But faith always operates in the present tense. It does not throw away our hope of heaven, but it does focus on what God has provided for us in this lifetime. Faith will not work if our focus is always on what is ahead of us. We can use it to experience victory today and for eternity. I believe this is what John is telling us in 1 John 5:4.

My focus was on faith alone in my early years. This caused me to ignore hope, which had the unintended consequence of causing faith to become ineffectual in my life. Manifestations of God's power were few and far between, happening only by accident. I have observed others who have fallen into the same trap over the years. Those who pursue the so-called faith message tend to go all in on faith. They ignore hope and vision without realizing that by doing so, they are committing themselves to a life of struggling to walk in the faith given to them by God. You may have fallen into this trap, but you can break free just as I did. The Holy Spirit is waiting to help you. All you need to do is acknowledge His presence and ask for His help.

Hope Stealers

I have briefly mentioned my personal struggles with understanding the faith message. The hurdles that were most difficult to overcome were the traditions I had been taught at the church my family attended when I was a child. It was an old-fashioned denominational church, and the ministers believed God piled suffering, lack, and sickness on us intentionally. They did not believe that there was a need in the modern church for the Holy Spirit or His gifts. I had to attend catechism classes in my eighth-grade year and remember our teachers telling us that Jesus came to guarantee an eternity for us with God. We were also told that He would expect us to suffer throughout our lives in order to earn the right to enter our future reward.

My sister developed cancer in her senior year of high school. I remember the pastor praying for her to have strength through the battle. He never once prayed for God to heal her. Our mother had been exposed to the message of healing at some point thankfully. She taught the high school Sunday school class but was fired for telling them that God would heal my sister. He did and she now has three beautiful children who would not be alive if we only had our church to depend on.

My childhood church is no different than many churches today. Ministers attend seminary where their minds are filled with religious tradition. They emerge with a desire to serve God but no revelation of truth. These men and women fill pulpits each week teaching their denominational beliefs that often run contrary to Scripture. Without realizing it, many will fall into the trap that my childhood pastor fell into. They mean to provide comfort but unwittingly become a tool in Satan's hand used to steal hope from God's children.

Apathy Is the Enemy of Faith

Apathy is one of the greatest enemies of faith. It is the fruit that grows from a hopeless heart. Many people have left the church in this condition, having had their hope stolen by their minister, members of their congregation, or any number of life events. This grieves me. Christians should be dealing hope to those who are hopeless. Unfortunately, this is not always the case, and some of the worst hurts occur in churches. In my experience, it requires an intervention by the Holy Spirit to break the power apathy holds over a person.

Losing hope is the first step toward a hardened heart. It can happen to any of us. I believe this is why we are told in Proverbs 4:23 to keep our hearts "with all diligence." In other words, we are the guardians of our hearts. The choice is ours alone to make about what will (and will not) be allowed to enter our hearts through our eyes and ears. This is a truth many Christians do not understand, which explains why they sit week after week in services listening to ministers who are not preaching from a place of revelation.

I have heard ministers stand in the pulpit proclaiming God uses sickness and disease to humble His children, or that He no longer heals people today. No wonder so many people have lost all hope! I am thankful for churches where the truth is preached, they are in the minority. You might wonder how we find them. The answer is by cultivating a relationship with the Holy Spirit and allowing Him to lead us.

One of the key tactics Satan uses to destroy a person's hope and vision is religious tradition. You must always be on guard against this. I cannot recommend opening your Bible highly enough to refer to every verse that's cited when listening to a sermon or reading a book such as this one. The Holy Spirit was sent to lead us into all truth (John 15:12–15), and He is living inside of your spirit if you have made Jesus your Lord. He will help you protect your heart if you are willing to let Him.

You may be wondering how this applies to operating in God's measure of faith. We have seen in this chapter that hope always precedes faith. If Satan is successful in stealing a person's vision, they will lose hope and have no target for faith to focus on as a result. We see in Romans 15:4 that the Word of God will minister hope to our hearts, and this is one of the reasons I have mentioned making meditation in the Word a part of your daily routine. The Holy Spirit is with you and will guide you on this journey. He was sent to reveal Jesus to us, and, with His help, I believe you will live your life to the fullest, walking in the faith of the Son of God.

Chapter 12

Finding Hope in God's Word

Where there is no vision, the people perish:
but he that keepeth the law, happy is he.

PROVERBS 29:18, KJV

After our discussion in the last chapter, I believe you have a much clearer picture of the ways that religion destroys hope. Jesus told His disciples that the traditions of men render the Word of God powerless in our lives (Mark 7:13). I used to wonder why, but the Holy Spirit showed me that faith can only tap into His power when it has a target to aim for (hope). Satan knows this. He uses our traditions to steal hope so there is no foundation for the faith of God to operate in our lives. The only way to guard against this is through daily meditation in the Word of God and fellowship with the Holy Spirit.

An Alcoholic Finds Freedom

Let me illustrate the point I am trying to make with a story of an alcoholic who once confronted me after a chapel service in a street mission. I was a volunteer in their recovery program and had preached the message the night this encounter occurred. The man was homeless and waiting for me at the back of the chapel. His story surprised me. He had been in the chapel several months before and had heard me quote Romans 1:16, where we are told that the Word of God is the power of God. This man decided to prove Scripture was powerless when he left the service that night. He went to a local liquor store, bought a bottle of wine, and sat down to drink. The mission staff had given him a Bible, so he pulled it out. He randomly selected the book of Philippians, read the first verse of the first chapter and took a drink. Nothing happened, so he read the second verse and took another drink. He continued with this pattern of reading a verse and taking a drink until he passed out. When he woke up, he repeated the process with a new bottle. The next morning, he found he would throw up at even the smell of alcohol! The Word of God had taken root in his heart and set him free completely from his alcoholism.

The one common thread I observed among the men in that street mission was that they all lacked hope. Most were homeless and suffering from any number of addictions. Satan had robbed them of any hope. I mentioned Romans 15:4 at the end of chapter 11. It reads, "For whatever things were written before were written for our learning, that we through the patience and comfort of the Scriptures might have hope." While I was volunteering with the street mission, I did not have the revelation of hope I have today. However, the Holy Spirit used this verse to start me on my journey. He led me to teach the men very basic fundamentals of the Christian faith. This was a departure from the normal approach of preaching salvation messages in every chapel service. Although I did not understand what was happening, the Holy Spirit used those messages to begin ministering hope to the men. Things did not change overnight, but we started to see men radically changed by the power of God. The Word of God was taking root in their hearts and ministering hope to them. Scripture was taking root and releasing God's power in their lives, just as it had for the alcoholic who confronted me that night after chapel service. Men were freed from additions, reunited with their families, and given a new start to their lives.

God Has Not Called Us to Just Cope

The men we ministered to in that mission had mostly been on the streets for years. Some had even grown up homeless and knew nothing else. They had no hope of ever seeing anything more in their lives. Unfortunately, many Christians live in a similar state of hopelessness. This does not mean they are homeless or dealing with an addiction like the men in the mission. Instead, they are stuck in hopeless jobs or are suffering from sickness or disease with no hope of deliverance. The only thing that keeps most of these people coming back to church each week is that most everyone else is living similarly hopeless lives.

I want you to know that God does not expect you to just cope with your issues, sicknesses, and problems. He wants to minister a revelation of the hope of your calling (Ephesians 1:18) into your spirit. The primary vehicle carrying this revelation is His Word. The alcoholic found deliverance accidently by continuously reading Scripture. I am not advocating you do what he did and take a swig of alcohol after reading each verse! I am saying, though, that you will never experience more until you make a commitment to meditate daily in Scripture. Change won't occur overnight, but as evidenced by the story of the alcoholic, it will happen if you do not give up.

Miraculous Power Can Be a Catalyst for Hope

I have met people like the alcoholic whose testimonies inspired me to hope for more than I was experiencing in my Christian life. Some shared stories of miraculous deliverances and others miraculous healings. I believe Paul understood the power of miracles to foster hope when he wrote 1 Corinthians 2:1–5:

And I, brethren, when I came to you, did not come with excellence of speech or of wisdom declaring to you the testimony of God. For I determined not to know anything among you except Jesus Christ and Him crucified. I was with you in weakness, in fear, and in much trembling. And my speech and my preaching were not with persuasive words of human wisdom, but in demonstration of the Spirit and of power, that your faith should not be in the wisdom of men but in the power of God.

His primary goal in ministry was demonstrating the power of God. He knew people needed hope, but most would not receive his teachings without a demonstration of the miraculous. Paul set a very high bar for us to follow. We have the same Holy Spirit he had, which means we can reach the same heights he did. I don't believe God is holding back His power from us; rather, He is only waiting for us to make the commitment to His Word.

You Can Reach for More

You may not be called into the ministry, but you can walk in the miraculous. We see an example of this in Acts 6. Stephen was chosen to serve as a deacon, but he still did great signs and wonders (Acts 6:8). How did this happen? Acts 6:8 tells us he was "full of faith and power." We have already seen that faith must have hope to stand on, so it is inferred that Stephen was also a hopeful man. I believe he hoped to see the Holy Spirit manifest and developed an internal vision of this happening in his soul. Faith connected to this vision and the power followed. You can follow his example and walk in the same power he did. It all begins with ministering hope into your spirit through meditation in Scripture.

Hope Is the Starting Point

As I've mentioned previously in chapters 9 and 10, the key to finding hope and releasing our faith is to turn off the things that pull our attention away from the Word of God. The big question for us is how hungry we are to experience all God has ordained for us to walk in. Are we hungry enough to fast a season of our favorite sitcom or sports team? My struggles with the faith message were not answered until I first became willing to turn off my television, computer, and social media accounts to sit quietly with the Holy Spirit. He helped me each step of the journey, and I found that my hope began to increase as we spent more time together fellowshipping in Scripture.

I hope you are starting to see that everything begins with meditation. The enemy has made this a dirty word that's typically associated with mystic religions and cults. For myself, meditation is simply fixing my focus and attention on something like a single verse, passage, or chapter in the Word of God. Oral Roberts once shared a story in a meeting I was in that illustrates the process of meditating on Scripture until it creates a picture in your soul that will activate the faith of God in your life.

Reverend Roberts' early ministry was not marked by the miraculous manifestations and tent meetings that he became known for. The story I heard him share occurred while he was pastoring a small country church. This was a typical country Pentecostal congregation with very minimal demonstrations of power. He became hungry for more and started to set aside time to seek God earnestly. The Holy Spirit led him to read through the four Gospels and the book of Acts three times consecutively on his knees over a period of thirty days. He obeyed, and it was during this time of intense meditation in the Gospels and Acts that his hope for the miraculous birthed a vision of himself laying hands on the sick, casting out demons, and raising the dead. This vision activated faith, and a worldwide ministry followed.

You are the only one who can choose to pursue Scripture or remain bogged down in religious tradition. Oral Roberts chose the former and immersed himself in Scripture until he could see himself standing before Lazarus' grave and commanding him to live. We can do the same thing Oral Roberts did. We can seek the Spirit for direction on specific areas of Scripture to meditate on. He may lead us to the Gospels and Acts, as He did for Oral Roberts, or to just a single book or passage. The keys to achieving the miraculous are a readiness to obey the Spirit's leading and an eagerness to immerse ourselves in Scripture until we can see ourselves possessing everything promised.

Chapter 13

Meditation on the
Word Gives Birth
to Hope and Vision

*"But you say, 'If a man says to his father or mother, "Whatever profit
you might have received from me is Corban"—' (that is, a gift to
God), then you no longer let him do anything for his father or his
mother, making the word of God of no effect through your tradition
which you have handed down. And many such things you do."*

MARK 7:11–13

I once heard Charles Capps tell a story in a sermon that I believe
will help us better understand the place of hope. Reverend Capps
spoke of a man who lived in a cabin out in the woods. This man lived
without the modern conveniences you and I take for granted. There
was no electricity or running water, and the cabin floors were dirt.
The man attended church one hot Sunday. He paid no attention to
the temperature in the room until a cool breeze suddenly started to
blow on him from a duct in the ceiling. He had never experienced
anything like that and thought a miracle had occurred! The man
stopped an usher when the service ended to tell him about his experience. Surprised by the man's claim of experiencing a miracle, the
usher told the man that someone had adjusted the thermostat to
lower the temperature in the room.

The man had never heard of a thermostat. It sounded like a miracle device to him. He asked the usher where he could get one. The usher directed him to the local hardware store. It was open on Sunday afternoons, so the man stopped and asked for a thermostat. The store clerk helped him pick one out. He bought it and promptly attached it to the wall of his cabin, just as the one he had seen at church was attached. But there was a problem with the setup. This man had never heard of air conditioning and did not understand that the thermostat could not cool his home on its own. It is designed to set the goal (i.e., temperature) for the air conditioning system.

I know this is a simple analogy, but it helps us see the relationship between hope (the thermostat) and faith (the AC system). Just as a thermostat cannot produce cool air on its own, hope also cannot produce anything in our lives without a connection to God's measure of faith. Faith is the victory that overcomes the world (1 John 5:4), but it must have a target in place for us to experience this victory in our lives. Like the thermostat, hope provides faith with a goal to shoot for.

Faith Requires a Vision

Jesus told His disciples that believers would lay hands on the sick and see them recover (Mark 16:15–18). Can you see yourself doing this? The power of God will not flow through you to heal the sick until you do. This image can only be developed through constant and continuous meditation in God's Word. I recommend reading verses like these in Mark 16 over and over. Close your eyes and try to picture seeing the sick recover after you lay hands on them. It will take time to renew your mind in this way, but the result will be much more powerful than if you run out and start praying for everyone you encounter.

We have already seen that God ministers hope to us as we meditate in His Word (Romans 15:4). Hope will always proceed vision. Vision is an internal image in the soul. Faith will not function in the absence of hope and vision. You must see yourself in possession of what you are hoping to receive from God in order for faith to become the substance of it.

I once heard a story about a pastor's wife who had very poor eyesight. She had been prayed for by some well-known ministers and had given up on ever receiving healing. A healing evangelist visited the church, and she avoided him in order to keep from being embarrassed by yet another faith failure. He finally cornered her on the final night of meetings and asked her to take her glasses off so he could pray for her. She had no expectation and prepared to be disappointed once again.

The minister prayed for the lady and asked if she could see. He told her to keep her eyes shut when she started opening them. This confused her, but she kept them closed as directed and he asked again if she could see. Once again, she tried to open her eyes only to be stopped by him. This was starting to frustrate her, but the Holy Spirit interrupted her thoughts. The Spirit directed her to spend a few minutes praying in tongues as she pictured herself seeing without her glasses. She obeyed and, in a few minutes, understood what the minister was asking. A picture began to emerge in her soul as she prayed. At first it was cloudy, but as she prayed and focused on the promise of healing, it became clearer. She suddenly could see herself without the glasses and shouted. It was at that point the evangelist commanded her to open her eyes. Everything in the room was clear, and she had perfect vision! A miracle occurred that night because one minister understood the importance of visualizing possession of a promise before manifestation comes.

What Do You See?

You can apply the principles in this book and see results just as the pastor's wife did. The key is how you view yourself. Can you picture walking in divine health and prosperity? Do not let Satan discourage you if you can't. You have the power to change your internal image. The Holy Spirit is with you and will guide your steps. He will show you passages to meditate on and minister hope as you spend time obediently focusing on them. Never forget that your internal picture is a direct reflection of the things you have been looking at and listening to. If you do not like what you are seeing, change the input! It really is as simple as that.

I mentioned Proverbs 4:23 in chapter 11. We saw in the verse that it is our responsibility to guard our souls. How do you know if you are effectively guarding your heart? I have found the best gauge to determine this is my internal image. If I see myself sick and suffering, then these things will manifest in my body. If I see myself healed and whole, faith will cause alignment in my body even if it is currently suffering from some type of symptom. Take a moment and close your eyes. Ask yourself if you can see yourself walking in divine health or needing a vaccine when we move into the flu season. If you see yourself needing a vaccine, you need to change your dominant picture. Doing so will require focusing your attention on the healing promises found in Scripture, such as 1 Peter 2:24 or Psalm 107:20.

Hope Is Our Legal Guarantee in the Court of Heaven

Christians often struggle with faith because they lack hope and vision. Hope cannot exist in the absence of God's Word. We have already seen in Romans 15:4 that hope is ministered to us by Scripture. The Greek word translated as "comfort" in this verse represents a personal exhortation providing evidence that will stand in God's court. Do you remember in chapter 10 when we saw that faith is "the substance of things hoped for" (Hebrews 11:1)? The word "substance" represents a legal title showing ownership. Hope is birthed from

Scripture due to the assurance that the promises we are meditating on are legal guarantees that will always produce a verdict in our favor in the courts of heaven.

Meditating on God's Word

We have seen that hope is ministered to our hearts through meditation in Scripture. This requires a commitment to turn everything else off and focus solely on the Word of God. Christians often struggle in this area because they have allowed themselves to be distracted by the noise of this world. I referenced a part of Paul's prayer in Ephesians 1 previously but would like to look at the whole prayer:

> Therefore I also, after I heard of your faith in the Lord Jesus and your love for all the saints, do not cease to give thanks for you, making mention of you in my prayers: that the God of our Lord Jesus Christ, the Father of glory, may give to you the spirit of wisdom and revelation in the knowledge of Him, the eyes of your understanding being enlightened; *that you may know what is the hope of His calling*, what are the riches of the glory of His inheritance in the saints, and what is the exceeding greatness of His power toward us who believe, according to the working of His mighty power which He worked in Christ when He raised Him from the dead and seated *Him* at His right hand in the heavenly *places*, far above all principality and power and might and dominion, and every name that is named, not only in this age but also in that which is to come. (Ephesians 1:15–21, emphasis added in first half of verse)

Paul prayed for God to open the spiritual eyes of those he ministered to. He wanted them to see the promises of God with their spiritual eyes and receive a vision of "the hope of His calling." The Greek word translated as "calling" refers to God's invitation to salvation and all His blessings. We see some of these promises listed at the beginning of Ephesians 1:

> We are blessed with all spiritual blessings in Christ Jesus (v. 3).
>
> We were chosen by God in Christ Jesus to be holy and stand before Him without blame before the foundation of the world (v.4).
>
> We were predestined to be adopted into God's family by Jesus (v.5).
>
> We were made to freely partake of His grace in Christ Jesus (v.6).
>
> We have been redeemed and been forgiven of all sin according to the riches of God's grace through the blood of Jesus (v.7).
>
> We have access to all God's wisdom and understanding through Christ Jesus (v.8).

I recommend using this list as a starting point. Replace the word "we" with "I" to personalize each promise. This is a great starting point for developing your habit of meditating on Scripture each day. You can expand the list with other verses as the Holy Spirit points them out to you. To get the full benefit of this exercise, you must not forget to shut everything else off. This includes your mobile phone. In my experience, those who ascend to the highest levels of revelation knowledge are fully committed. They are not satisfied by a once-a-week service and instead make the pursuit of God's Word their highest priority.

Chapter 14

Exercising Active Patience to See Manifestations

My brethren, count it all joy when you fall into various trials, knowing that the testing of your faith produces patience. But let patience have its perfect work, that you may be perfect and complete, lacking nothing.

JAMES 1:2–4

I have discussed my past struggles with faith and explained that they largely occurred due to my ignorance of hope and vision. The Holy Spirit helped me recognize this. He spent some time teaching me about hope and then asked me to look at patience. Patience is a critical aspect of walking by faith that is often either ignored or misunderstood by Christians. I personally had been so focused on understanding faith that I had never really spent any time studying patience.

I fully endorse the need to teach faith, but we must look at the whole picture and not just a single piece. For example, there are Christians who are trying to operate in their measure of faith while living an ungodly lifestyle. They may accidentally stumble into a few faith victories every now and again, but they will never go further without first cleaning up their life. This is why we need to look at the whole picture and not just one or two parts of it. The faith message reminds me of a puzzle. Faith represents the outer edges, but there are a lot of pieces that are not edge pieces. These are needed to complete the puzzle. Hope, vision, and patience are examples of pieces that are often missing in our puzzles.

Faith and Patience

The author of Hebrews tells us that we can only inherit God's promises by exercising faith and patience. He also tells us that patience is needed for those who desire to receive God's promised blessing (Hebrews 10:36). Jesus also mentioned the need for patience in His explanation of the parable of the sower in Luke 8:15: "But the ones *that* fell on the good ground are those who, having heard the word with a noble and good heart, keep *it* and bear fruit with patience."

Patience is another critical aspect of operating in the measure of faith. I would go so far as to say it is just as important to faith as hope and vision are. Scripture ministers hope. Hope motivates us to continue meditating on the promise until it becomes vision. At that point we will be able to see ourselves in possession of the promise, and faith will begin to operate and work toward bringing the image in our soul into full manifestation. Patience is the force that we exercise once faith is activated, and then full manifestation occurs.

Letting Patience
Have Her Perfect Work

I believe James 1:4 is one of the boldest statements I've found in Scripture. It reads, "But let patience have *its* perfect work, that you may be perfect and complete, lacking nothing." This verse tells us that those who let patience work through to completion will be "perfect and complete, lacking nothing." There are very few passages in the Word of God that promise us anything close to this. Patience is a vital part of operating in faith, but it is also something that most of us are ignorant about.

The Greek word for "perfect" is more accurately translated as either "fully mature" or "completing all necessary stages to reach the end-goal." According to James 1:4, you will not reflect either of these ambitions without first letting patience complete its work. Let's think about the implications of this. If you or I are lacking any good thing in our lives, it is because we are not allowing patience to operate. Can you see why we can't afford to ignore it in our pursuit of faith?

What Is Patience?

I found that patience was not what I had thought it was. In my mind, it was an empowerment to endure the trials and afflictions of life with grace. In other words, if I was sick or exhausted, patience would enable me to show up at church with a smile on my face. The Holy Spirit had to correct my thinking. He helped me see that patience is not passive. It is active. One of the best definitions I have heard is that patience is faith that is active over a period of time. It is an active resistance against the attacks of Satan that seek to cause us to let go of our faith. Patience will remain active until victory is achieved.

A lot of Christians have no issue with attending service, having their faith stirred through the singing and teaching, and then experiencing immediate manifestation. These same people will begin to falter, though, when the manifestation does not occur immediately. They have God's measure of faith but lack patience. For example, if an altar minister prays for you to receive healing and you wake up the next morning feeling no better, what would your reaction be? The majority probably would think the prayer did not work and give up on being healed. Standing until the manifestation comes requires us to exercise patience.

The dictionary defines patience as calm endurance or perseverance. Perseverance is an active word. A person operating in patience will endure through any trial or affliction to victory. They will not bend or bow to the devil's strategies. But you will never reach this point if you are not first grounded in the Word of God.

I have heard people say they are "enduring their sickness." It is not uncommon when visiting people in the hospital to find them with their feet up, popping pills and watching television. God is often far from their mind until the preacher shows up. They may say they are being patient, but what they are doing is not actively exercising patience! You may not agree, but I don't see the benefit of sitting mindlessly in front of the television instead of listening to messages on healing and meditating on the Word of God. You cannot feed on the corruption of this world and expect to see the measure of faith operate in your life.

James tells us to submit to God and resist the devil (James 4:7). The word translated as "resist" in this verse is a military term that refers to strongly resisting the enemy. It is not passive. You cannot resist the devil when you are lying flat on your back, submitting to the symptoms in your body. There are people who will push back on what I am saying. Most argue that they have done everything they can and are just waiting on God to heal them. We have already seen in 1 Peter 2:24 that God has already provided healing in Christ's redemptive work. Healing has already been provided, but we must aggressively seek it using the measure of faith while exercising patience.

Patience Is Not Passive

When we are lying around in bed complaining about our symptoms, we are not exercising patience. I learned this lesson through a scolding given to me once by the Holy Spirit. He was not angry with me but did seem a bit frustrated. I had woken up with a high fever and was lying in bed complaining because the fever did not seem to be responding to me. I was confessing the Word, playing messages, and listening to an audio Bible. The Holy Spirit interrupted me. He asked me one question: "Why are you blocking faith from being able to operate?"

A person operating in faith would have gotten prayer and then immediately began to plan as if the symptoms were not present. They would be full of confidence and tell everyone they met that they had received their healing. Faith and patience are both very aggressive. A person operating in the measure of faith will refuse to quit. Patience empowers them to stand as long as necessary without becoming discouraged or quitting. The person who successfully operates in faith over a prolonged period without wavering is the person who has tapped into the power of patience.

Will You Stand?

A lot of people will successfully release small doses of faith. They are not able to endure. I once heard someone talk about the way they started out running marathons. He stepped out of his front door on his first full day of training filled with enthusiasm and confidence that he could run a full marathon, and he ran with all his might as far as he could. He eventually collapsed to the ground and described the pride he felt at giving it his all—until he looked up and realized he had only made it as far as the end of his driveway before collapsing! I don't know if this actually happened, but his story does illustrate the need for patience in our Christian journeys.

Many Christians are just like this man. They hear a sermon or read a single verse and get all excited about what they have heard or read. Their excitement prompts them to launch out in faith, believing for the world. These people are motivated by excitement and will usually not stand for more than an hour before giving up and declaring faith did not work for them. This will be our story if we attempt to step out in faith without first becoming deeply rooted in the Word of God.

Faith, hope, vision, and patience all require us to be deeply rooted in the Word of God. If you will take the time to develop deep roots in the Word, you will stand as long as necessary without wavering. There are a lot of people sitting in church week after week who are not committed to the Word of God. They are satisfied and stuck. These people have never developed in the measure of faith given to them by God. We must become grounded in Scripture and develop deep roots for faith to mature into patience.

The person who is undeveloped in patience will usually not stand for long. When it comes to our prayers being answered, it may take only a split second or it may require years. You can shorten the time required for the manifestation by increasing your commitment to God's Word. For me, there are things that used to take what seemed like forever to manifest that now manifest almost instantaneously in my life. I have grown in the Word, and I know you can too. You can operate in the measure of faith and overcome any attack the enemy throws at you. The first step is to set aside time, open Scripture, and ask the Holy Spirit to introduce Himself to you.

Chapter 15

Activating Faith by Following Enoch's Example

Jesus saith unto him, Thomas, because thou hast seen me, thou hast believed: blessed are they that have not seen, and yet have believed.

JOHN 20:29, KJV

There are many people in the church today who refuse to believe anything they cannot see. Unconsciously, they are choosing to follow the path of Thomas. Jesus told Thomas that those who can believe without seeing would be blessed (John 20:29). As we discussed in chapter 8, the Greek word translated as "blessed" provides us a picture of being moved into an enviable position. God has given you the measure of His faith. You will be in an enviable position if you choose to activate it. Doing so requires a commitment to spend time meditating in Scripture and fellowshipping with the Spirit every day.

The devil will use every weapon available to get you to renege on your decision to pursue the Word of God above all else. We spoke in chapter 14 about the need to actively resist Satan. Faith is an attitude. It does not operate in our emotions. It is a spiritual reality and force that operates out of our spirit. When we release it, it will stay on the job and continue to work until it moves the mountain that is standing in our way if we do not waver and turn our eyes away from God and His Word. If you remain immovable from the Word, you will see the manifestation of the thing you've released faith for.

Faith Is a Lifestyle

You do not have to wait for a critical diagnosis from a doctor or a financial crisis to activate faith. The Holy Spirit has helped me understand the need to actively use the measure of faith He has given me and make it the controlling force in how I live and conduct my life. In fact, I have found that most of my faith failures were a result of only using faith when a problem manifests. I liken this to a weight-lifter who only uses their muscles when they are needed in a competition. If they do not have a regular training regimen, the likelihood of them being able to lift record-setting weights is very low. In the same way, if you do not develop a training regimen in the Word of God that you follow each day, you will struggle to use faith to overcome a crisis when it hits.

You can develop yourself spiritually to the point where releasing faith becomes as natural as anything else you do. Doing so will require effort. There will be a price to pay, but I've never met anyone who regretted paying the price required to operate in faith. If you will make a commitment to do whatever is needed to grow into the measure of faith given to you by God, you will also grow into the place where you will be able to overcome anything that Satan throws your way. I believe you would not have read this far if you were not willing to make this commitment.

Faith Is Spiritual Substance

Faith is not a tangible, physical force. Hebrews 11:1 tells us that it is spiritual substance. The measure of faith given to us by God operates from our spirits. If we activate it, it will continue to operate unless we stop it. We see an example of this in 2 Kings 13:20–21:

Then Elisha died, and they buried him. And the *raid-ing* bands from Moab invaded the land in the spring of the year. So it was, as they were burying a man, that suddenly they spied a band of *raiders*; and they put the man in the tomb of Elisha; and when the man was let down and touched the bones of Elisha, he revived and stood on his feet.

We have already seen in the account of the centurion that God's measure of faith was available prior to the cross. Elisha was a prophet who operated in it. Faith was such a part of his life that it even infused his bones to the point that a dead man was resurrected when thrown into his grave. The man's dead body touched the prophet's bones, and the power of God flowed. Elisha's bones radiated faith even after death! Faith has not lost its potential and can do the same thing today if we will just believe.

Elisha ministered under the old covenant. He lived before Jesus' death, burial, and resurrection. He was not born again, and he operated in ministry as a spiritually dead man. The measure of faith was not available to him like it is to us today. It operates in the spiritual realm. He was restricted to his soul and body and yet still walked in the power of God. Can you imagine the power of God's faith flowing from our spirit compared to the faith that infused his bones? I am not sure any of us can really comprehend it.

Releasing Faith through the Laying on of Hands

Paul tells us the Spirit who raised Jesus from the grave to life lives in our spirits (Romans 8:11). He also tells us that the Holy Spirit exercised the mighty power of God in the resurrection of Christ (Ephesians 1:19–20). He dwells in the spirit of every Christian, which means we have the mighty power of God in our hearts. It can also be transmitted to others. A person with revelation knowledge can do this by laying their hands on another person and releasing the power already in their spirit. You can purposely activate the measure of faith and transmit its power through your hands.

Faith is governed by spiritual law (Romans 3:27) just as electricity is governed by natural law. I have observed that it operates in the spiritual realm similar to how electricity does in the natural realm. Your hands can conduct the power of faith just as copper can conduct electricity in the natural realm. We must discipline ourselves to not just lay our hands on people haphazardly. We must press into prayer to allow time for the Holy Spirit to train us how to use our hands to release God's power like a mechanic uses their tools. You should not lay hands on another person until you are ready to release the power of faith. The Holy Spirit will show you how to prepare yourself to do this.

Enoch Operated in Faith

Enoch operated in faith to the point that he did not experience physical death. He drew so close to God that he was translated directly into His presence. He lived under the old covenant, and we live under the new. I have often wondered what would happen if we developed the same level of intimacy with God as Enoch had. The Holy Spirit has told me the answer to this question is found in the faith that Enoch operated in. Hebrews 11:5–6 describes that faith for us:

> By faith Enoch was taken away so that he did not see death, "and was not found, because God had taken him"; for before he was taken he had this testimony, that he pleased God. But without faith *it is* impossible to please

Him, for he who comes to God must believe that He is,
and *that* He is a rewarder of those who diligently seek Him.

In the following sections we will examine three elements of Enoch's faith listed in these verses. First, we must believe that God exists. The second element is seeking God, and the third is trusting that God rewards His children. We must engage in all three to activate the faith God has placed in our spirits. His faith will not work with only one or two. Without all three, we will not be able to operate in the measure of faith and we will not minister in His power.

Do You Believe God Is?

The first element of Enoch's faith is that he believed God existed. A person who has not heard the gospel message will not know about Him (Romans 10:14). They will not have any basis to believe He exists. They will have no foundation on which to develop a relationship with Him. This principle applies to our entire Christian journey. Every belief begins with knowledge. I once heard a minister define a belief as a firm persuasion based on knowledge. The Holy Spirit has expanded this in my heart to include knowledge gained in relationship. Taken together, we can define a belief as a firm persuasion based on knowledge gained in relationship with the Word of God and the Holy Spirit. Enoch developed a relationship with God that spanned more than three hundred years (Genesis 5:22–24). His faith grew out of his relationship with God. We will also grow into the measure of faith given to us by God in accordance with the depth of relationship we develop with Him.

A lot of people have been deceived into believing they are operating in faith. They have been told that all they needed to do was believe in God. The problem with this approach is that our belief in

Him is only one element that is required to operate in faith. Faith will not work until it is acted on completely. James provides additional insight into this for us:

> You believe that there is one God. You do well. Even the demons believe—and tremble! But do you want to know, O foolish man, that faith without works is dead? (James 2:19–20)

Satan and his minions believe in God. I have met very few unbelievers who do not believe He exists. Neither Satan, his minions, nor unbelievers can activate the measure of faith. It is not enough to just believe in God. If it were, we would see unbelievers operating in the same measure of faith as believers. There are three required elements that must be present for faith to work. Believing in God is only one of them.

Are You Diligently Seeking Him?

The second element of Enoch's faith that is listed in Hebrews 11:5–6 is seeking God. Enoch sought God for more than three hundred years before his translation. There are people who believe in God but have never put Him at the forefront of their life. Many only serve Him to ensure they escape eternal damnation. He did not save us to give us a proverbial "get out of hell free" card. He desires to build a relationship with us, and this will not happen if we are unwilling to spend time with Him. You must make a commitment to seek God every day to operate in His faith.

We have spoken at length in previous chapters about the distractions in the world today. They are used by Satan to distract us from our relationship with God. I encourage you to start paying attention to what you are doing with your time. You cannot operate in the measure of faith if you spend more time with your television than you do with the Word of God and the Holy Spirit. If you are spending eight hours each day at work, two commuting, two with your family, and four watching television, you will have no time left to spend with God or His Word.

God Rewards His Children

The final element of Enoch's faith listed in Hebrews 11:5–6 is trusting that God rewards those who diligently seek Him. We must believe God exists, seek Him, and then believe that He will reward us for doing so. Faith will not work without all three of these elements. I believed in God and was seeking Him but struggled to believe He would reward me for doing so. It did not seem that I was worthy. The Holy Spirit used Hebrews 11:5–6 to show me that this was the issue I was having with faith. I was missing one of three required elements because of my perceived lack of worth for God to be able to bless me. The Holy Spirit helped me understand that my position in Christ Jesus qualified me to receive from God. Questioning God's willingness to reward me was equivalent to questioning His Word. I could not get His faith to work in my life until I first corrected this. I've made the correction in my life and know you can too. You can activate the measure of faith in your spirit and become a conduit of God's power.

Chapter 16

Grace and Faith

*For by grace you have been saved through faith, and
that not of yourselves; it is the gift of God.*

EPHESIANS 2:8

As we move forward, it is important to remember that faith cannot operate independently. This is true of all biblical truth. We must consider the whole of Scripture and let the Word interpret the Word. Faith operates hand in hand with grace. Neither is a more important truth than the other. Unfortunately, a lot of error exists in the church today because whole segments have separated themselves into either the faith camp or the grace camp. Both camps utilize truth but also will lead us into error if they are not joined. One minister we listen to describes himself as belonging to "the crack camp" because he attempts to always stay in the crack between the faith and grace camps to maintain balance.

Salvation By Grace and Faith

The church I grew up in emphasized God's grace over faith. Our pastor often quoted Ephesians 2:8, claiming Paul tells us we are saved only because of God's grace. He argued that we had no choice in the matter and only those selected by God to be saved would have His grace extended to them. He was wrong. God extends His offer of salvation to anyone who will accept it. It is because of His grace this offer is made. It is through the measure of faith given to us by God that we can accept it.

We receive the measure of faith from the Word of God and then use it to receive salvation. As we have already seen, God does not take back His faith once we are saved. He expects us to continue to use it to conduct our lives (Galatians 2:20). While I recognize the need for books such as this one and teaching messages, these must never replace the time we spend meditating on Scripture and fellowshipping with the Spirit. He will use teachers like me to help you grow quicker, but you still must open the Bible and put your eyes on verses quoted in messages for yourself.

The Holy Spirit helped me understand this truth with an example from my family's dinner time while growing up. I have an older brother and sister. Do you think it would have been practical for me to have them describe what they had eaten at supper instead of sitting down and eating? This is exactly what many Christians do. They allow the ministers they listen to eat at God's dinner table but never sit down to eat what He has prepared for them. Just as a person cannot survive in the natural realm without eating, we also cannot survive in the spiritual realm without partaking of God's Word for ourselves.

With this in mind, let's look again at the first part of Ephesians 2:8 which reads, "For by grace you have been saved through faith…" This verse is not telling us that we are saved only by grace. It is also not telling us we are saved only by faith. Both faith and grace are involved in salvation. You cannot choose one over the other. Salvation is available to us because of God's grace but received only through His measure of faith. As I said in the previous paragraphs, it is the combination of grace and faith that opens the door of salvation for humanity to walk through. Grace provides the offer and gives faith the ability to accept.

It Is Not Grace or Faith

I was never a stellar student as a child, but I do remember some of my lessons. One science class in particular. It involved the two chemicals sodium and chloride. Independently, both are poisonous. Sodium will kill a person if ingested in a sufficient quantity. Chloride will do the same. They are both poisonous independently, but when mixed, they become common table salt, which is needed for a healthy diet. In the same way, grace and faith are very potent spiritual forces. When they are mixed, salvation is produced. If we pursue one at the exclusion of the other, we will end up in a ditch on the side of the road. You must not forget that there are ditches on each side of the road you are called to travel in your Christian journey. I've seen people overcorrect when they found themselves in a ditch, only to end up in a ditch on the other side of the road. Our goal must always be to stay in the center of the road where we will avoid the ditches.

Technically speaking, we are saved by faith through grace—not by one or the other. There is a temptation to focus on a single truth and ignore others. Yielding to this temptation will lead you into error. "Error" is simply truth taken to an extreme in isolation of all other truth. No truth from God's Word can stand independent of any other. We are discussing God's measure of faith in this book. The Bible tells us faith works by love (Galatians 5:6), so we must also study love to understand faith. Love is the foundation on which God's measure of faith operates. Many people have gotten off track by pursuing faith and not love. In the same sense, many have gotten into error by pursuing faith while ignoring grace or by pursuing grace while ignoring faith.

What Is Grace?

I have heard so many definitions of grace. The most common one defines it as God's unmerited favor. It is something that God has done for us independent of what we deserved. Grace is simply a description of the things God has chosen to provide us in Christ even though we do not deserve them. Romans 5:8 tells us that God demonstrated His love for us in the crucifixion while we were still sinners. From this we see that grace is not performance oriented.

Grace is an extension of God's favor to humanity with no strings attached. It is offered equally to all because it is not based on our actions. I cannot earn more of His grace than you, and you cannot earn more than me. The level of grace received does not increase based on how good we are, and it does not decrease when we sin. Grace is totally dependent on the nature and character of God.

Titus 2:11 tells us, "The grace of God that brings salvation has appeared to all men." God's grace is offered to every person who will ever live. In context, this verse is talking about the grace that brings salvation. The grace of God expressed in the crucifixion of Jesus is available for every person who will receive it. First John 2:2 tells us that Jesus died for the sins of the whole world and not just for those who would receive Him as their Savior. The worst sinner who has ever lived had the price of their sin paid for just like we have had the price of ours paid for by Jesus in His redemptive work.

Grace alone cannot release the power of God. It must be mixed with faith. Faith is expressed in an action that is our response to the grace extended. I have heard people question why we are not seeing the power of God in greater manifestation today. They do not understand that God has already moved on our behalf. He is now waiting for a response from us regarding what He has already provided in Christ's redemptive work.

Let's use salvation to illustrate the point I'm trying to make. God has already extended an invitation of salvation to every person. This invitation will not be accepted by a lot of people. People leave this world destined to spend eternity separated from God in hell only because they do not accept His invitation to be saved. Jesus prepared hell for the devil and his angels. God has never sent a single person to hell. He did not intend it to become a destination for humanity. People are going there, though, because of rejecting His offer of salvation.

Peter tells us that God has provided "all things that *pertain* to life and godliness (2 Peter 1:3)." The provision comes through His grace. We could say then that grace has provided salvation, healing, deliverance, and anything else you or I will ever need. This provision is available, and faith is the vehicle we use to receive it. I told you that the Holy Spirit helped me understand faith with an illustration involving my family's dinner table in chapter 4. My mother would serve dinner, and it was expected that we would be there to eat. She took the time to set the table (grace), but we could not consume the food if we did not sit down at the table to eat (faith).

What Is Faith?

The majority seem to think faith is something we do to gain a response from God. For instance, regarding confession, it is often taught that if a person confesses the Word of God enough, God will respond and give them what is needed. I've also heard ministers say that if we pray correctly, He will give us what we need. Unfortunately, the majority think faith is an action taken to gain a response from God. I used to think this was the case, and I am thankful the Holy Spirit helped clarify my thinking.

In the simplest terms, we can define faith as our positive response to God's grace. The reason I confess the Word of God is not to get God to do something for me; rather, it is to declare my trust in His provision. For example, in the area of healing, I confess Scriptures such as 1 Peter 2:24 to declare that I really believe my healing has already been provided through the stripes Jesus received on my behalf.

Without realizing it, many Christians seem to have fallen into the trap of believing God will move on their behalf if they do something first. Some think they are required to pray, and others think they are required to confess Scripture before God will respond. They are not operating in God's measure of faith. His faith enables us to reach out and take what has already been provided, independent of our actions, through Christ's redemptive work. A person who thinks they will have to do something for God to move on their behalf is operating in legalism.

I struggled with faith for many years before learning these truths. The Holy Spirit showed me I was attempting to use faith in a way that was like a person using a pry bar to open a door. I was operating out of my natural being and attempting to twist God's arm to make Him give me the things I was believing for. There was not recognition in my heart that He had already provided the things I was seeking.

Faith Appropriates
What Has Been Provided

There are a lot of people who mistakenly believe they can use faith to force God to move. One of the most vital truths that we must never forget is that it is impossible to change God's mind or force Him to move on our behalf. Faith does not move God. This statement goes against the way a lot of people teach this subject. It is a foundational truth that must be established if our goal is to successfully operate in God's measure of faith. We cannot move God because if He has not already moved by grace, faith will not be able to receive. Faith can only appropriate what God has already provided by His own free will and will always be totally independent of what we have done or deserve.

God's measure of faith is simply the vehicle that we use to receive what has already been provided in Christ's redemptive work. We cannot receive anything that has not already been provided through His grace. Mark 11:24 tells us that we are to believe we receive when we pray. I have heard people use this verse to claim someone in their church to be their husband or wife. One of my classmates in

Bible school did this to claim a lady in the church choir as his wife. He went around telling everyone that he had received her by faith. However, there was a problem with his logic. She was already married. God would never allow us to use His measure of faith to take another person's spouse!

Faith does not move God. We cannot use the measure of His faith given to us to make Him do anything. It was given to us so we can receive what God has already provided. Understanding this one concept set me free from the struggles I had gone through in my early years of trying to learn how faith operates. Many people are just like me. They think they have activated faith in their life but are operating in a works-based mindset that will never enable them to receive the things God has provided. I believe you want to enter the rest of faith just as much as I do. You have come this far in the book, and there is no doubt in my mind that you will succeed and enter the fullness of all God has provided you walking in His faith.